A SELF-DEVELOPMENT PROGRAMME

Perfect presentations

Acknowledgements

It is somewhat difficult to know where to begin this list! But missing school days I have to acknowledge the army instructors at RMA Sandhurst, The Small Arms School Hythe who taught me to how to communicate effectively in both the classroom and the slit-trench! They must have made a fair job of it as I had the opportunity later to practise the art a plenty as a Regimental Training Officer, a Chief Instructor at Sandhurst and Team Leader at an Overseas Staff College.

After transferring these skills to the City of London I was influenced in discussion (and argument) over a ten-year period by many people, perhaps the most influential being:

Nigel Brown (then of Kingstree, now of Grant Pearson Brown Consulting)
Jeremy Francis of Rhema Consultants
David Gilgrist of The Learning Point Presentations School
Anna Cook of Ward Cook Associates
Nick Gray of Gray's Marketing Communications
Various tutors from Mast

All of these have either run courses and/or given me advice and help in preparing my own. All encouraged my interest in and knowledge of this particular management skill and I am grateful to them.

A SELF-DEVELOPMENT PROGRAMME

Perfect presentations

THE ESSENTIAL GUIDE TO THINKING AND WORKING SMARTER

John Collins

MARSHALL PUBLISHING • LONDON

A Marshall Edition
Conceived, edited and
designed by
Marshall Editions Ltd
The Orangery
161 New Bond Street
London W1Y 9PA

First published in the UK
in 1998 by
Marshall Publishing Ltd

ISBN 1-84028-133-2

SERIES CONSULTANT EDITOR
Chris Roebuck
PROJECT EDITOR
Conor Kilgallon
DESIGN
Balley Design Associates
ART DIRECTOR
Sean Keogh
MANAGING ART EDITOR
Patrick Carpenter
MANAGING EDITOR
Clare Currie
EDITORIAL ASSISTANT
Sophie Sandy
EDITORIAL COORDINATOR
Becca Clunes
PRODUCTION
Nikki Ingram
COVER DESIGN
Poppy Jenkins

Originated in Italy by
Articolor

Printed and bound in
France by SIRC

Video Arts quotes extracted from training films:

pp 12, 22, 43, 75: "I Wasn't Prepared For That"
p73: "Can We Please Have That The Right Way Round"

Contents

1

Introduction
Successful presentations
Types of presentation

Effective communication

The involved parties

Critical questions

Introduction

Every day of our lives we communicate, support, oppose or simply absorb ideas. Babies attract attention by screaming, while parents transmit calm and reassurance with soothing noises. Whether at home, school, university, club, sports field or office, we need to communicate with those around us.

We have to develop the ability to put our case in a way that stands the greater chance of success, and it matters not whether it is a plea for more pocket money, an excuse for late homework, a proposal of marriage or a million-pound merger bid. The process of attracting attention, communicating ideas and gaining the desired result is the same in every case.

In our daily life, most of us carry out this process with a reasonable level of success. We are articulate, interesting people – at least to our friends and family – and well able to keep "our end up" in classroom, family circle, bar and office.

When, however, it comes to speaking at a formal meeting or worse still, giving a brief before a group of people, some of us face a confidence crisis. Others have no particular fear of speaking in public, but are not prepared to put in the work that is necessary to do the job properly. For both groups the result is the same: a poor performance with the consequent loss of self-esteem.

Effective communication

To be successful in any environment there is a need to communicate effectively. This book will help you do just that by showing you how to transfer the skills you already use effectively in an informal setting to that of a more formal one.

Though the focus will be on formal presentation, the advice given can be adjusted to suit any situation. The formal presentation gives the opportunity to cover all the basic points of speaking in public, and the range of speaking opportunities we all have to face from time to time.

Though we will look at the tricks of the trade, the basic ingredient is "you" – your voice, your style and your personality. My main task is to show you how to continue to be "you" when talking to any group – and to give you the confidence to do so.

What is a successful presentation?

Think of a wonderful piece of music. A good speech or talk, no matter how long or short, is just like that. Not only does it have a beginning, a middle and an end – introduction, main body and finale – but it almost certainly contains a variety of passages. Some are quiet, contemplative, introspective; others are intriguing, exciting; some are simple, some grand and pompous, but all engage the emotions and intellect and leave the listener with a feeling of satisfaction. Just as there are many different kinds of music, so there are different types of presentation.

Whilst it may be stretching the point to suggest that a business presentation will create the same emotional impact as a symphony, the results in terms of wealth creation and job satisfaction can be of notable importance both for the individual and their company. Success will be the result of painstaking research, intellectual flair and the ability to sell new ideas in an interesting, and when necessary, an exciting way. (And probably a little luck as well!)

At a more basic level, the successful presentation of an idea or series of ideas or suggestions to colleagues will influence events and relationships and have an impact on a particular situation or the general success and morale of the team. At every level the following ingredients will be at play:

- You and your audience are clear on the aim or purpose of the event.
- You understand the needs of your listeners.
- You know your subject.
- You have planned your speech.
- You have rehearsed properly.
- You are confident in manner and style.

I make no apology for again stressing "you". For even though many presentations today are team efforts, it is the individual who holds the floor at any particular time and has the task of making an impact.

These issues are dealt with in some detail in the chapters that follow and all aimed at allowing you to project yourself in the best way possible. Success and enjoyment of this particular skill will have a marked influence on the way your business and social life develops.

Of course, presentations encompass many different events and occasions. These are outlined in the next section.

Types of presentation

The formal

Although it is a formal presentation that springs to mind when we think of public speaking, this is, in fact, the style least used. It is because the formal presentation contains all the aspects, skills and processes used in any other public speaking situation that it is the best example to use to explain and practise presentation skills.

A formal presentation is usually a speech or lecture on a specific subject given to a large audience. It can be introduced by a chairperson and is often one of a series at a conference or seminar. This is, in fact, the easiest presentation to give because the speaker is in control of the proceedings without much fear of interruption.

The informal

Nowadays most presentations in the business world are informal affairs with small groups who are encouraged to participate. The informal talk includes all the requirements of the formal one with the added pressure that the speaker should appear relaxed while still remaining fully alert and in control. The object of both the formal and informal talk is to add to the audience's understanding or knowledge of a subject. No specific action by the listener is required.

One-to-one

These are the most frequent presentation opportunities. It is essential that they are conducted as a conversation, but they can be formal or informal, depending on the status and needs of the other person. Many people do not count one-to-one as public speaking and because of this do not suffer the same anxiety as when faced with a group audience.

In fact, all the skills of a successful presentation are required and, because they must be framed within a conversational style, they are in some ways more difficult to apply. The successful speaker is one who can impress the listener with his personality and manner.

Briefings

Briefings usually cover a specific issue and are designed to tell the audience about a particular process or activity and their part in carrying it out. An effective briefing ensures that each member of the team fully understand the plan and their own role in achieving its success.

There must be plenty of opportunity for checking that the arrangements are understood and for questions – whether it is for a cup final, an office move or an assault on an enemy camp!

Workshop

At a workshop the audience are expected to contribute as much, if not more, than the speaker, whose main role is to facilitate the proceedings. The sessions are usually broken down into a series of mini-presentations, followed by group work and then probably suggested solutions.

The presenter needs to combine the skills of listener and controller with the ability to draw out and encourage the involvement of others while contributing his own knowledge.

Meetings

Meetings provide us with a great number of informal presentation opportunities – thankfully usually short ones! Many people fail to make the best use of these occasions by failing to follow the basics of good presentations, and end up disappointing themselves and their listeners – one of whom is usually the boss!

Telephone

Loss of visual contact (unless you have a screen) on the telephone prevents the use of many of the usual presentation skills but accentuates others. If you use the phone effectively you already possess the ability to present well, particularly on informal occasions.

Video-conferencing

This is used increasingly for business meetings but also for linking up lecture halls to a central speaker. Initially, the main advantage of this was the savings in travel costs. The value, however, of bringing groups together where they can see and react to each other to exchange information and ideas, no matter where they are, is also proving to be a major advantage. So the need for everyone to be able to present their ideas with skill is becoming more important. For the first-time user it is paramount that before going live, they have a practice run to see the effect that time delay has on both speech and movement.

The involved parties

...A presentation is a business equivalent of an open goal...

In a presentation there are three parties involved: you, the presenter; the audience; and the institution you represent. The way in which success impacts on all three is related, but different. For the presenter, a well-received speech increases self-confidence and esteem and contributes to the continued development of their business skills.

For the audience a good presentation is a pleasurable experience leading to a better understanding of the subject and increased respect for the speaker and the organization he or she represents. The institution itself can gain long-term benefits to its reputation; it can often also obtain short-term benefits if the presentation results in winning a contract.

The presenter

The good presenter may start off feeling a little "tight" and nervous, though confident that he has done everything to ensure success. As the speech progresses he can sense that he has established a good rapport with the audience. In the end, success will depend on whether or not the presentation has fulfilled its objective.

This is not necessarily the same as realizing that the event has "gone well" – that would only prove that your speaking skills were very good. For you be an effective speaker, the event must achieve its purpose.

The audience

The audience may come to the proceedings feeling either ambivalent or goodwilled towards the speaker. Most of them know why they are there, and what they want to get out of the event: some clear insights and ideas on the points at issue delivered in a clear, interesting and enjoyable way. At the end some of them ask questions and expect them to be answered in a friendly and worthwhile manner.

What they do not want is an overlong diatribe of incoherent facts that confuse rather than clarify, delivered by someone who is uninterested, ill-informed and, worst of all, arrogant!

The institution

An organization selects a speaker with varied emotions: confidence, trepidation, curiosity or sometimes real concern. It is the school, college or firm's reputation that is at stake, both in the long and short term.

If the speaker is an unknown quantity, those who chose him will be nervous at the start and ready to be moved to tears of anguish or joy as the performance develops! Your own experience of being in an audience has probably exposed you to these extremes. However, the good organization should become involved in the process long before the presentation to make sure that nothing but good comes out of it.

Critical Questions

Before you begin to work through this book, be clear of your aims for doing so. Are you really starting from scratch or just looking for some extra tips to add to your current skills?

You may find it useful to consider the following questions:

- When did you last make a presentation?
- What type was it?
- Did you feel confident before, during and after the event?
- Did it go well?
- Do you want/need to improve your skills?
- Are you prepared/do you have the time to work at your presentation skills?

Your answer to these questions may give you a reason to look at this book. If you are prepared to work at its exercises and follow its advice, it will help you to give perfect presentations in the future.

Summary

- While we all have the innate ability to communicate effectively in our normal lives, many of us find it difficult to transfer this skill to the public arena.
- A good speech has all the components of a great piece of music, and affects the listener's emotions in the same way.
- You need to consider yourself, the audience and the institution you represent when making a speech.
- You should be clear why you want to improve your skills.
- You should be prepared to make the time to do so. Setting aside practice time is very important.

2

Self-assessment
Why people perform badly

Self-assessment exercise

Action plan

Summary

Why people perform badly

Getting realistic feedback on your speaking skills can be a problem. As public speaking is universally regarded as an "ordeal", friends and colleagues are usually sympathetic after a performance and rarely give useful constructive criticism. Even when they do, it usually relates to a specific point or incident and fails to address the underlying causes of any perceived failings.

A useful ice-breaker on a basic presentation skills course is to ask the participants to be thoroughly negative and list all the things they can think of that contribute to a poorly delivered speech. Try this yourself before reading any further!

Invariably the list includes: rambling; lack of preparation; no humour; no aids; poor timing; too long; mumbled words; no eye contact; inaudible; too loud; confusing; was bluffing – not an expert; sarcastic; poor logic; too fast; too slow; waving arms; condescending; no theme; nerves; uncomfortable room; equipment didn't work; no questions; didn't answer questions; unrehearsed.

It is always easier to produce a critical list than a positive one, but if you turn the list on its head you have before you everything a good speaker aims for. Put the list into a logical sequence and you have the chapter headings (sometimes disguised) of every book on effective presentations:

- Preparation – of the talk and the location.
- Delivery – using voice and posture effectively and controlling nerves.
- Aids – designs and selection of equipment, and its use.
- Handling and answering questions.

Having identified the issues, the next stage is to ensure you can obtain feedback on how you are handling and hopefully improving on these aspects.

Unless you specifically ask a colleague to watch your performance with the aim of giving feedback and provide him with a system for doing so, it is unlikely that you will ever get more than generalizations and few effective proposals for improvement.

Probably the main benefit from attending a formal course or having individual professional help before a major presentation is that a trainer or consultant uses a checklist to identify a speaker's strengths and weaknesses in order to give constructive, logical criticism and advice. The list enables the consultant to review each specific skill or attribute in turn and how they have influenced the overall effectiveness of your speech. Provided you can persuade a colleague to use such a list they too can give effective feedback and help you to decide whether you need professional help or just more practice.

Self-assessment exercise

Use the checklist below to assess your current general skill level at presentations, meetings and one-to-one sessions.

You can also use the list to assess your performance, using a variety of criteria, at a specific presentation you completed recently. In this case, ask a colleague or friend who attended your presentation to give you their feedback and make their assessment of your skills, too.

Preparation	Yes	Not really	No
Was your aim clear to you?			
Was it clear to your listeners?			
Did you research your audience?			
Were you clear what they wanted from you?			
Did you really know what you were talking about?			
Had you done sufficient back-up research?			
Did you organize your talk into a logical sequence?			
Did you link your themes to give a "flow"?			
Had you checked the location and the equipment?			
Did your aids work?			
Had you rehearsed effectively?			
Had you thought about the Q & A session?			
Delivery	**Yes**	**Not really**	**No**
Did you feel nervous: before?			
during your speech?			
Did you control your nerves?			
Was your stance confident?			
Do you feel your voice carried well?			
Did you speak, not read?			
Did you use words for the ear or the eye?			

Self-assessment exercise

Delivery	Yes	Not really	No
Did you use, to good effect: rhythm?			
speed?			
volume?			
pause?			
Did you maintain good eye contact?			
Did you use gestures effectively?			
Did you keep your enthusiasm throughout?			
Did your opening work well?			
Did the question and answer session go well?			
Did you finish on a high?			
Did you use your notes/script effectively?			
Did you develop a good rapport with the audience?			
Did they react and involve themselves?			
Did the humour work?			
Did you enjoy the session?			

How did you score?

Have a careful look at your scores. Consider in turn each of the aspects that need improvement. Did it go wrong because:

■ You don't know how to do it – you need training.

■ You can't do it (you think) – you need training.

■ You didn't plan carefully enough – you need to organize yourself more effectively.

■ Your notes weren't good enough – your organisation must improve.

■ You didn't rehearse enough – you need to organize yourself better.

It is also important to think about the good points and what you can do to make them even better.

If the list of points for improvement is long, it is best to work on these by training. If you can, attend a course, where you will get the opportunity to practise and gain confidence in a non-threatening environment.

The great thing about presentation skills courses is that you are guaranteed to improve your performance.

What cannot be guaranteed is that the improvement will be sustained. Sadly, it often is not, because people forget to apply the two vital ingredients practised on every course: careful preparation and rehearsal.

Another option is to use a consultant for one-to-one sessions. These are particularly useful if you already have some experience and need to work on a specific presentation. Although you lose the chance of rehearsing with others, being able to focus on your script and delivery can produce excellent results.

If you prefer to learn from books, fine. Reading alone, however, will not make you a good performer – you have to practise.

If the areas for improvement are not too many, make an action plan focusing on a few issues at a time.

Action plan

To prepare an action plan, simply take a blank sheet of paper and head it: "To improve my impact at presentations during the next month I will..." Then add three sub-headings: "Stop", "Start" and "Do more of". Then list under each, the things you should stop doing at your presentations, the things you should do and the things you would like to expand on.

The following chapters focus separately on these issues and show how effective preparation, practice and rehearsal will help everyone to control their nerves, project their own personality and deliver great presentations.

On my courses I always focus on the delivery issues first. By doing this, the problem of nerves can be dealt with very quickly and individuals begin to relax as the points are discussed. It also means that when focusing on preparation, that session can be broken down into its three main parts and then presented to the group, giving the chance to practise both elements. I have followed that practice in this book so that you can, if you wish, also practise each stage.

Summary

We know from our day-to-day conversations that we all have the ability to speak effectively with enthusiasm and vigour, particularly on a subject that interests us. The issue is transferring this innate skill to the public or group forum.

Understanding what makes a good or bad speech and being able to assess your own performance is the first step to improving your standard and ensuring that you can confidently prepare and deliver a perfect presentation.

Remember, a good speaker must:
- Know the truth of his subject.
- Be able to analyse and synthesize.
- Be able to organize and arrange material.
- Know audiences and how they react to different appeals.
- Believe wholeheartedly in what he says.

PLATO

3

The basics: delivery
Overcoming fear
Body language, the voice, notes and location

Mnemonics to remember

Words and humour

Preparing prompt cards and OHPs

Overcoming fear

...If you know your subject, you can give a presentation...

Do you have what it takes to stand and deliver? Or do you embarrass both yourself and your colleagues when you make a speech? Do you feel frustrated at the end of a meeting or briefing session when you know you had an important contribution to make, but you failed to carry your colleagues because you didn't make your case effectively or, worse still, didn't make your case at all? So, what makes an effective speaker. As we saw in Chapter 2, the list includes:

- Control of nerves.
- The voice.
- The right words.
- Use of body language – non-verbal communication.
- Prompts, scripts and notes.
- The right location.
- Useful aids.

The right combination and control of these ingredients enables you to deliver an effective, confident talk with impact. Understanding each one and, where appropriate, maximizing the way you use it, improves your delivery skills. Continual review will lead to continued improvement. Let's look at each one in greater detail.

Control of nerves

We all feel some nervousness before we "perform". If you don't have a surge of adrenaline pulsing through your veins before a meeting or speech, it can only mean you are insufferably arrogant (there are some!) or the occasion is not important to you. Nerves are not the issue – it is their control that matters.

Luckily for most of us these tensions are not severe, though they are worrying and can detract from our performance. These anxieties can be overcome. Merely ignoring our fears and hoping the problem will go away is not the solution. Briefings need to be no-nonsense, interesting, accurate business advice delivered in a way that is easily understood and believable and which demonstrates your good faith, integrity, common sense and knowledge. Indeed, for the businessperson the creation of a rapport with the audience and confirmation of integrity will be 80 percent of the task. This does not mean your presentations should be dull, uninteresting affairs – quite the contrary should be the case – but they are a business or social skill, not an artistic performance.

The fundamental skill for controlling tension is to:

■ **Know your subject.** You will soon be found out if you don't know what you are talking about. Your listeners are there because they believe you can give them some useful insights and increase their understanding of the issues. If you are trying to bluff your way through, this will quickly become obvious and the mounting tension between you and your audience will eat into any self-confidence you thought you had. People do not have to agree with what you say but they do expect your arguments to be based on a fair knowledge and understanding of the subject. You must be prepared to read and research thoroughly before preparing a speech and to make sure that you are in all respects up to date.

No book on presentation skills can help you with this fundamental issue: YOU MUST KNOW WHAT YOU ARE TALKING ABOUT!

■ **Understand the basics of speaking to groups.** Here, the book can help by showing you how to structure what you say and how to involve the listeners. To help your audience to concentrate on and to enjoy the presentation are fundamental skills that can be learned and improved with practice.

Knowing your subject and understanding the basics of speaking to groups will give you confidence in your ability to influence others effectively. This confidence will overcome your fear of failure and, coupled with one other essential ingredient, will produce increasing success. This essential ingredient is:

■ Practice
■ More practice
■ Rehearsal
■ More rehearsal

This practice not only includes rehearsing the script and the management of your aids, but also by making time to review your presentation style and the administrative arrangements. By now you will have a growing understanding of your own strengths and weaknesses and it may help to review the relevant parts of this book to refocus on these issues.

Some people are so nervous that they never speak at meetings, never accept the task of leading or briefing – though they should because they often have more to contribute than the pushy overconfident "good speaker" who is always ready to give his/her views at length. For these people the tightening of the throat, the thumping heart, banging knees, blushing face and sweating brow are all good reasons to stay hidden in the crowd.

We are more comfortable being one of a group. Once we step outside it and become the focus of attention, we risk condemnation or criticism. It does therefore need some "nerve" to take the first step to overcome and control our apprehension.

Overcoming fear

Breathing and breathlessness

Overcome the feeling of breathlessness and a thumping heart by achieving control of your breathing. Follow this simple routine a few minutes before you begin your presentation:

- Stand or sit quietly.
- Pause for a minute.
- Begin consciously to pull a deeper breath in through your nose.
- Pause for a second or two.
- Slowly let the breath out through your mouth with a long "phew".
- Repeat this 3 4 times, increasing the depth of in-breath, pause for 3–4 seconds and lengthen the "phew" as you breathe out.
- Don't overdo holding your breath (this will prevent the uninitiated or unpractised from fainting!).

This simple form of exercise is practised by actors, athletes and successful presenters – anyone who needs to calm themselves before a performance.

Believing in yourself

Convincing yourself that you are confident is very important psychologically. So before a performance in front of the boss, the audience, the team, look in the mirror and, smile and say a couple of times in a good loud voice, "This is going to be very good!"

Providing you do not break into helpless giggles I defy you not to feel more comfortable about your speech. Even looking slightly ridiculous will cheer you up!

You can usually find a good time to do this before a meeting. The lift is an excellent venue for this strange but effective bit of personal psychology!

Preparation

If you know you have prepared well and rehearsed successfully, a heightened sense of anticipation of the action to come replaces your jangling nerves. (But more of this in Chapter 4.)

Practice

If you are working on a team event, a good preparation plan (see p46-47) will include at least two rehearsals (after the script has been agreed). But if you are new to or nervous about your performance and want to ensure the basics are right before the main rehearsal, then practise:

- In front of the mirror.
- In front of a family member.
- In front of colleagues or friends.

Do not simply read the script/notes silently to yourself. To practise delivery and increase your confidence you must speak aloud as though an audience were present.

Know your opening by heart

Knowing the first few lines is a great confidence booster. It helps to calm the nerves to be able to speak the first few lines without the worry or distraction of looking at your notes. An opening that works well and gets things off to a good start is a good buttress for your self-confidence and tension control. Be sure to speak fairly slowly to start with so that the audience can tune in to your voice. Use your voice effectively from the start.

The voice

Most of us do not need to develop our voices but we do need to understand how to use effectively the voice we have. The larger the room and the audience, the greater the need to project our voice in the best way. Remember the comparison with a piece of music – it is the voice that interprets the score.

The mnemonic R S V P P is a useful memory jogger for the best use of the voice.

R　Rhythm

S　Speed

V　Voice

P　Pitch

P　Pause

Rhythm

A speech given at a single pace without variety of tone will quickly either dement or anaesthetize an audience. There is a need to inject an ebb and flow, a rise and fall into the voice, to bring the sounds to life. There are times when short staccato sentences create the right rhythm, at others the words should flow as the emphasis requires.

This is difficult to practise out of context but try listening to Shakespeare or a heavyweight politician in debate. Rhythm has a direct link with speed.

Speed

A lot of nonsense is written about speed of delivery. True, the Americans still believe it is more dynamic to talk fast, but the real trick is not the speed per se but speed variation, hence the link to the rhythm. Varying the speed makes for interesting listening and helps maintain concentration. So, cover the easily assimilated passages at a brisker tempo and give time for the complicated ideas to be understood by using a more deliberate, steady pace.

To tell a story you need the excitement of speed, while explaining the intricacies of "fixed option" to a "green graduate" calls for a more measured delivery. The speed also needs to match and correlate to the volume you are speaking at.

Volume

Volume level depends on the size and shape of the room you are using. It is, however, also important to use volume for emphasis, and to command and hold your audience's attention by raising and lowering the volume of your delivery.

Many potentially good speakers fail to impress because they speak too softly for too long. "Speaking up" tends to slow the pace and helps you to vary the volume more clearly. However, once you have captured your audience's attention, you can have them on the edge of their seats by carefully lowering your voice – particularly if you are telling an interesting story or giving good advice!

Pitch

Pitch is the ability to "throw" your voice so that you can be clearly heard in all parts of the room. It is difficult to explain and requires a practical demonstration. Try inflating your chest and raising the sound from your chest to the back of your throat or top of your head. Open your mouth wider than usual and raise your voice (not the same as shouting). One of my teachers used to say: "Let the words BOUNCE OFF the walls."

You cannot pitch your voice – or do anything much with it! – if you barely open your mouth to let the lucky words escape. If you do not use your mouth and lip muscles properly, you will produce a dull monotone. Get your lips, mouth and jaw working actively to accentuate words and enunciate them clearly.

To prepare for a speech you should warm up so that the face muscles are relaxed and the throat is clear. The best exercise (the loo, en route to the meeting is a good place to practise

this!) is to go through the vowels four or six times really working the mouth and jaw as much as possible to stretch the muscles. This will loosen your face (and smile) muscles and help you to pitch and enunciate in a clear and interesting way from the start.

Pause

Finally the pause. Practised properly this becomes the most effective use of the voice, though most of us ignore it. In a television interview, Harold Macmillan once explained the "point of the pause" something like this:

"When you make a speech you must only make one or two points – possibly three, never more. Of course you dress it up this way and that with a story, a fact or explanation, with humour, with solemnity but always on that one (or three) point. And vary the pitch, but above all, remember the pause... if you can do it... it is the most effective way of emphasizing your point."

Count to five

To be effective, a pause needs to be at least to the count of five. This will seem to you like an eternity. Unless you practise you will quickly lose your nerve and end up with a pause so short that it goes unnoticed by your listeners.

The voice: exercise

Read the following passage through normally. Draw a line at three points (not necessarily at the end of a sentence) where a pause would give effect. Now practise reading it and counting up to five out loud at each pause. The second time count to yourself and look carefully at your audience; do not stare at your notes or fidget! The silence is scary, isn't it?

"From aft came the tunes of the band. It was a ragtime tune. I don't know what. Then there was 'Autumn'. I went to the place where I had seen the collapsible boat on the boat deck, and to my surprise, I saw the boat, and the men still trying to push it off, I guess there wasn't a sailor in the crowd. They couldn't do it. I went up to them and was just lending a hand when a large wave came awash of the deck. The big wave carried the boat off. I had hold of an oarlock and I went with it. The next I knew I was in the boat." (From *The Titanic: The Wireless Operator's Story* by Harold Bride).

Many speakers fill what should be pauses with "er" and "um", or "well then" or "you see". Filling the space in this way is a sign of nervousness and a device to gain "thinking" time for the next phrase. This destroys the rhythm of the talk and robs the listeners of the break they need to absorb what is being said.

Speakers are usually blissfully unaware of this irritating habit and, unless their best friends tell them, they will continue to spoil good speeches with these hesitant noises. It is surprising, though, how quickly this mannersim can be eliminated once you are aware of it. The improvement in style and self-confidence is remarkable.

Find out what your "er" count is by asking a friend or checking a video of yourself to see how many "er"s or "um"s you make a minute. You may be surprised at how high the total is. Make up your mind that you are going to stop this bad habit. Remember to:

- Speak a little slower.
- Practise listening out for the "er"s when you are talking.
- Mark your script at frequent intervals with your "No 'er'" sign.

Another mnemonic:
If R S V P P doesn't suit you, try this old military one:

C Clear: the use of simple, easily understood words and phrases.

L Loud (enough): it is important that everyone can hear you.

A Assertive: A bright and confident air born of knowledge of the subject and good preparation.

P Pause: It is essential to allow the listeners to digest what you have said.

The right words

What you say and how you say it is always the key to a successful presentation. The aim here is to speak naturally for the listener not the reader, for the ear not the eye.

Make sure that your original script or your briefing notes encourage you to to talk naturally, using words which are easy to understand, appealing to the ear and sound right. Good grammar is not absolutely essential. When we speak we don't always complete our sentences, and we use words, phrases and slang which would be inappropriate on the printed page. Your speaking style during your presentation should reflect this.

A useful tip is to use the sound-bite mnemonic to provide a structure, to give a short sharp answer to a question, to make a point or to develop an argument. This is:

P State your position or make your point.

R Give a reason or reasons for this.

E Give at least one example or explanation.

P Restate your position or point.

For a sound bite you would probably give only one reason or example to support your case, but you could build on it as part of your argument when persuading your audience.

Here is an example of a sound bite:

Position:
I support the Charities Aid Foundation...
Reason:
Because it is an easy and tax efficient way to donate to charity...
Example:
By using the special CAF cheque book I can keep control of both spending and fund allocation...
Position:
So for me support of CAF is the best way to give...

Exercise

Try your own sound bite PREP by talking about:

- Your pet hate.
- Your favourite sport or hobby.
- The most useful business book you have read.

Humour

Wit and humour will add spice to any conversation or talk provided that it is immediate, reactive, topical and either is, or appears to be, spontaneous. However, it is not something that you can learn from a book as it is such an individual thing, and its style and manner is utterly dependant on the personality of the speaker. But points worth remembering are:

- Make fun of yourself, not your audience. It is better to tell stories against yourself which both amuse the audience and let them know you are human than to pick on individuals or specific sections of the audience.
- Do not continue to try to humour an audience who are unresponsive. If the jokes are not getting a laugh, change your style.
- Avoid joke book humour, originality is best, using amusing personal experiences. This does not mean that you should not tell jokes you have read elsewhere, but they must be relevant to what you are saying.
- Smile, but do not over-react to your own joke. If you are lucky enough to get a good laugh, make sure you pause to let your audience settle down before you continue with your presentation.

- Always relate humour to the matter in hand. The days have long since gone when presenters started off with "have you heard the one about..." and then related a poor joke which had nothing to do with the presentation subject. A good crisp joke, however, firmly related to the subject does help to get you off to a good start.
- Don't overdo your witticisms. Frequently, an inexperienced speaker, buoyed up by the "success" of his humour, will spoil the effect by overdoing the humour and begin to irritate some sections of the audience.
- Get your timing right. Whilst this applies to anything we say, it is essential when jokes are being used. The badly delivered punchline will embarrass you.
- Spontaneous, off-the-cuff remarks that occur to you as you talk, often in response to an unscripted comment, are the best type of humour. Take advantage of the moment. Some speakers have knack of reacting well in this way. You will soon learn if you have this gift. If you have, use it, but don't overuse it. If you haven't, stick to your script!

But you will not be surprised by now if I say that the key to successful planned humour is: PRACTICE!

Body language

The understanding of both your own and a listener's body language is an important skill for the effective speaker. It is important not only to spot those who are nodding off, nodding in agreement or merely shaking their heads in sheer disbelief at the comments you are making, but also to interpret correctly the more subtle signs. They might include making notes, doodling, leaning forward, following your movements or, returning eye contact.

Your own body language is important and, whether you are sitting or standing, can either support, be neutral or detract from what you are actually saying.

The issues to consider are:

The stance: standing

Whatever stance you adopt it should give a confident pleasing impression. It is best to start square to your audience, feet comfortably apart and balanced, your hands forward, one probably holding your notes. Without wishing to sound too militaristic, the old sergeant major's "head up, shoulders straight, stomach in" is good advice.

Unless you are trapped behind a lectern (or hiding there!), try to move around a little. Indeed it becomes essential to move if you begin to suffer a bout of knee shaking. Stay rooted to the spot and it will only get worse.

Move about and you will find that it will immediately stop.

This firm but relaxed stance gives a good impression. What a stark contrast with those who stand with hunched shoulders and crossed arms, shifting from foot to foot with eyes firmly rooted on notes, ceiling or floor!

Hands

For many observers it is the hands that create the pleasure or the pain. Good hand movement is a valuable aid to a speaker, but poorly used hand movement is merely a wasteful distraction. In fact, recent research from the Massachusetts Institute of Technology suggests that the natural hand movements accompanying speech are as crucial as the words themselves and that unless they support what is being said the listener will not receive the message.

For most of us it is natural to use our hands to emphasize a point when we talk. In conversation with small groups this adds interest, excitement and informality, but these movements, which tend to be short and flow with speech, are a distraction when addressing larger audiences.

With larger groups it is best to be sparing with gestures, but ensure that they are "grand" enough to be noticed or the audience will miss them. You may find it helpful to check your script

Body language

The objective is to include all your audience in your talk. This is not done by constantly sweeping the room with your eyes, row by row, but by fixing your gaze on one person in a group of listeners, and talking to him for a while before moving on to another group. Ten to 15 seconds with each group works well and everyone in the area of your contact will think you are looking at them (remember how often actors in a play seem to be talking directly to you).

If you need a confidence boost, it can be helpful to pick out a friendly face – particularly in the early stages – but you must also include the "enemy" some of the time!

or notes to see when a gesture would be appropriate. Mark the place with your gesture sign.

But don't overdo this technique and become a manic arm waver!

The stance: sitting

When you first sit down, sit right into the chair with your back firmly against the support. Sit square to the table with forearms resting easily on it. Sit up straight without feeling forced and plant both feet firmly on the ground about twelve inches apart.

This position gives an alert, friendly and confident impression and compares favourably with an individual slumped in a chair. Placing the feet firmly on the ground usually prevents the incessant jiggling of hyperactive foot-tappers – an irritation to anyone close enough to observe it and an indication of extreme nerves, boredom or arrogance.

Hands

Even when you are sitting, the hands are a useful aid. It is always best for them to be in view, with the wrist or

part of the forearm resting on the table – not under it. The gestures may not be so grand, but used sparingly they are effective in attracting attention or making a point. Provided you are not leaning forward all the time, doing so occasionally is a useful way to signal an important point or to attract attention.

Pockets

Speakers often ask whether or not they should be relaxed and put their hands in their pockets. The answer is: both, never; one or the other, it depends! Provided you don't end up playing with your kcys or coins, a hand in the pockct does create a more informal style and can help relax the audience. However, choose the right occasion – hands-in-pockets junior executive may not create the right impression if the audience are the main board.

The eyes

Everyone knows about the importance of eye contact but many of us feel some embarrassment trying to maintain it.

Sitting round a table at a meeting it is important to focus most (but not all) of the time on the individual you need to impress. However, do not ignore the others. If you find it difficult to look at someone directly or you are beginning to feel embarrassed, pick a point above the nose in the middle of the forehead and one either side of the mouth and move in a disjointed way between them. This breaks the feeling of staring at the same point the whole time.

Just because the book says maintain eye contact, it doesn't mean you must fix an individual with a manic gaze and never let your eyes leave their face! Don't feel eye contact must be constant. Both parties need the space to turn away and look elsewhere. Vary your gaze, from your notes to the face, to the OHP (overhead projecter) and to the side.

Some of us unconsciously fix our eyes about three feet above our audience or look out of the window for inspiration – anywhere but at our listeners! This is a sign of nervousness and can become a bad habit (you should spot it at rehearsal). To overcome it add a special sign to your note prompts to remind you not to do it.

But by far the easiest way to lose eye contact is to talk to the image thrown on the wall by your slides or OHP. You cannot maintain eye contact with your back to your audience. More of this when we consider the use and misuse of aids (see p62-77).

Mannerisms

Mannerisms are at best an irritation but at worst can lose the contract! Of course some of us may be afflicted with a physical disability that cannot be avoided, in which case we have to carry on anyway. If our techniques are good we will usually win the sympathy and support of the audience.

One of the best speakers I ever heard had a stutter. Initially, this provoked a feeling of unease in the audience, but he was such an accomplished presenter that soon the audience was actively engaged in willing him to find the word and enjoying the moment when he did. It was one of the most effective demonstrations of the power of the pause I have ever heard and I am totally convinced that some of the time he did it on purpose for effect!

Do you scratch, pull at your hair, or moustache or earring, or jangle the keys or coins in your pocket? To avoid irritating habits you must first be aware that you have them! If your best friend won't tell you then a video will. Once you have identified them, focus on stopping them by including a visual or text prompt at various points down the sides of your script.

Making this conscious effort of noting the bad habit and giving yourself the odd reminder not to continue doing it nearly always produces a cure.

Notes

We all want to avoid standing in front of an audience with a sheaf of papers in our hands waiting to be read. Provided your preparation has been thorough, all you need to deliver, with style, a speech that sounds spontaneous and creates a rapport with your listeners is a well-planned memory jogger.

Memory joggers are usually written on small cards 10 x 8 cms, if you are standing, or on A4 paper, if you are sitting. The cards should have a hole punched in the top right corner (left if you are left-handed) and be secured with a ring clip.

It is wonderful if you can give a talk without the use of notes. But this skill requires considerable practice and most of us do not have the time nor the ability to memorize a lengthy script and to deliver it as though it were off-the-cuff. Professional speakers may be able to do it but business people have many other priorities besides public speaking to focus on. It is best, therefore, to develop a technique that reminds you of what you want to say and helps you to say it effectively – using cards. An example is opposite.

Completing the cards

The cards should not be completed until the script has been drafted, preferably in full, though the more experienced or frenetic may do this in note form (see p47). The script should be honed to perfection in spoken English and then broken down into bullet points. The next step is to read it through a couple of times, underlining the words that will best remind you of what you want to say. These should then be written in large bold letters on the cards, using one card for each heading or sub-heading.

For example, one of the cards in my briefing notes for a presentation skills talk to junior executives looks like the card on the opposite page. This is card number five, as denoted in the bottom right-hand corner of the card.

It is made up as follows:

"Experience/Practice" is a repeat of the last line on the previous card (number four). By repeating it here (in lower case letters) it helps to move from one point to the next more easily.

Showing "VOICE" at the bottom of the card, in capitals (and repeated at the top of card number six in lower case letters) tells me that the next topic is a main heading.

"Overcoming Tension" is the main point here and my draft script has sections on "Breathing" and "Believing in Self", which are not dissimilar to the theme of this book. The words "Smile", "Say It" and "signs" are sufficient to jog my memory of what I wish to say on these particular points.

Similarly the headings "Prepare" "Know opening by heart" and "Rehearse" are sufficient to jog my memory on what I want to say on those subjects, with the additional reminders of practising in front of the "Mirror" and with "Friends".

In addition to the jogger points, add instructions to yourself and any warning notes down the right-hand side of the card, preferably in different colours to the main points. For example, use green for instructions such as VF3 (show video film 3) and red for things to avoid, such as "ER!", to watch your "er" and "um" count as you are speaking.

Experience/Practice

OVERCOME TENSION
- BREATHING
- BELIEVING IN SELF
    - SMILE
    - SAY IT
    - SIGNS...   VF3

PREPARE
KNOW OPENING BY HEART   ER!

REHEARSE
- MIRROR
- FRIENDS

VOICE   **5**

Notes

Some advise that the script or diagrams written on the OHP itself should be the memory joggers. This can work, particularly for experienced speakers or for those who have had to cut corners in their preparation. It can, however, be dangerous for the inexperienced speaker who may often spend too much time talking to the machine or the screen instead of to his listeners. In this system, the sides of the OHP are used for writing instructions or action hints on the right-hand side of the card and speaking bullet points on the left, thus avoiding the use of jogger cards. The subject of the OHP is giving a presentation on the use of the voice. The topics for discussion are printed in the middle of the card (rhythm, speed, volume and so on).

On the left-hand side are the joggers that will help me illustrate my points. Thus an example of how an orchestra works will help me describe the importance of rhythm. On the right hand side, abbreviations indicate that video film 6 will be shown, eye contact will be made and an example of a practice exercise will be given (the third one during the talk).

OHP diagram from a presentation on use of the voice

Orchestra	**Rhythm**	VF6
Fast/Slow US/UK speeds	***Speed***	Eye
loc/bodies soft/listen clap with authority	**Volume** **Pitch**	Prac3
Macmillan	**Pause**	
Don't use one	**Microphone**	VF7

Reading

When a script is unavoidable

If you are invited to read a speech verbatim direct from a script, decline if you can.

If, however, it is unavoidable, then accept that to do this effectively is a specialized skill and needs plenty of practice. Of course the modern way is to use a tele-prompt – though even this needs practice both for you and the tele-prompt operator. But, unless you are a sought-after speaker at a major conference, you are unlikely to be offered this excellent aid.

If you read a script (a long quote, a manuscript or a technical paper) you must make every effort to ensure that the delivery is not a dull, flat monotone but contains all the best elements of our RSVPP. This can best be achieved by the following routine:

- Read the paper through a number of times until the sense is clear to you.
- Read it again aloud to get the feel of how it sounds.
- Have the script reprinted in 16 point and double-spaced with the last sentence or phrase at the bottom of a page reprinted at the top of the next in italics.
- Go through it again highlighting key phrases and words.
- Put slash marks at the end of each sentence and phrase where you need to make a deliberate pause.
- Practise delivering to your audience putting the right emphasis on the important points and check that you have the right pronunciation for any difficult technical words.
- Decide which parts can be delivered at reasonable speed and which must be slowed down – a particularly important part of RSVPP when you are reading a script, as the tendency will be to speak too fast.
- Mark the places where you can break away from the prepared script to insert examples or anecdotes to show the listeners that you are not an automaton.
- Practise maintaining as much eye contact as possible. As you become familiar with your script, use the pauses to do this.

If you do not achieve the standard you want by following these tips, then you need the help of a specialist who will teach you the specific techniques of reading a script.

Location

You will rarely have much say in the choice of location, but following a few basic rules will ensure you make the best use of your particular pitch.

- **Room**
  Will it comfortably seat the expected number of attendees?
  What is its shape?
- **Seating**
  What style seating layout is best for the presentation?
  Formal conference, large number = theatre style.
  Workshop = tables with sufficient space to allow audience to face the speaker when required.
  Teaching/discussion, small group = U-shape best, boardroom table acceptable.
  Short briefing, small group = semicircle, no tables.
- **Lighting**
  Does the room have good daylight?
  Is the lighting banked so that the screen area lights can be switched off if necessary without plunging the whole room into darkness?
- **Power**
  Location of power points and distance from equipment.
- **Equipment**
  Check condition, serviceability, type. Can OHP take both landscape and portrait?
  When will you be able to rehearse?
- **Facilities**
  Is there space to place back-up and handout materials?
  Is there an area for refreshments?
- **Distractions**
  Are there people from other meetings gathering outside or nearby for their coffee break?
  Is there building work either in or outside the building?
- **Break-out room**
  Do you need extra rooms for discussion groups?
  What extra equipment is needed in each?

In many cases it will not be possible to check these things before the meeting, but to avoid a potential disaster it must be done before you start. Once you begin, anything that goes wrong is your fault, whereas before you do, it is the host's responsibility. Of course it will be of little use asking the Chief Executive if the OHP has a spare bulb, but there is usually someone around who can answer your questions.

Aids and questions

Two other skills – handling questions and using aids – are vital aspects of effective delivery. Not only do they require the practise of all the other delivery skills outlined in this chapter, but also a number of specific additional techniques. They are looked at in Chapters 5 and 6.

Summary

All the issues discussed in this chapter affect the quality of your delivery. They can be summarized as follows:

Delivery

The fundamentals

- Know your subject
- Understand the basics of public speaking

Nerves

- Control your breathing
- Believe in yourself – you are the greatest!
- Know your opening

Body language

- Relaxed, balanced stance both standing and sitting
- Hand movements to emphasize the main issues
- Eyes for contact, control and rapport

Voice

- Rhythm – ebb and flow
- Speed – change to suit
- Volume – quiet and loud for effect
- Pitch – vary it
- Pause – use it!
- Mannerisms – know what they are so as not to use them

Words

- For speech, not reading, PREP will help
- Notes: cards if standing, A4 if sitting, or, if you prefer, mark your OHP
- Reading: don't!

Attention to these points ensures a successful result provided that you have PREPARED, PRACTISED and REHEARSED your talk.

4

The basics: preparation
Structure plans
The beginning, the middle and the end

Fail to prepare, prepare to fail

The six questions

Feedback

The basics: preparation

"FAIL TO PREPARE – PREPARE TO FAIL."
"ONE MINUTE OF EFFECTIVE TALK NEEDS 30 MINUTES OF CAREFUL PREPARATION."
"THE TROUBLE WITH IMPROMPTU TALKS IS THAT THEY TAKE SO LONG TO PREPARE."

Do you believe the statements above? Do you apply their logic to your current system of presentation preparation?

Preparation is undoubtedly the most neglected area of presentation skills in all forms of public speaking, and, surprisingly, the business presenter is often a major culprit.

Most professional people are well-educated, intelligent and relatively articulate speakers who quickly learn and develop the skills for speaking to both large and small groups. This coupled with a deep knowledge of their subject convinces them that they present well enough to be successful with other professionals. This somewhat arrogant approach results in minimal preparation, either because business people do not consider it necessary or do not have, or will not make, the time for it.

In order to prepare a perfect presentation at a major event, the essential steps outlined below should be followed to the letter. If the occasion is of limited importance short cuts can be used.

What is the aim?

Before writing a word the presenter must be clear not only about the subject of his/her talk but, even more important, what its purpose is. This is not the same as the subject. The subject might be "Next Year's Mathematics Syllabus", or "The New Production Cycle", or " An Analysis of the Brewing Industry".

The purpose or aim can vary greatly, depending on whether you (or more likely your boss or sponsor) wish to persuade, inform, amuse, educate, inspire, motivate, teach or entertain your listeners on the matter. (Of course, a good speech combines many of these aspects, but it is vital to understand the *essential* purpose.) Before you start your presentation, you must be absolutely clear what the main objective is.

Frequently the aim is set by a superior or agreed by a group of colleagues. It can be a prescription for disaster if the boss is not himself crystal clear on what he wants to achieve. Vague briefs without specific aims inevitably lead to a well-prepared presentation being ripped to bits at the first rehearsal as the boss reworks your script to fulfil the requirements he should have made clear to you at the outset! To avoid this, do not hesitate to ask him to write his aim down or write it yourself and confirm it with him before you begin preparation.

Getting your objectives clear

Although this can cause irritation, it is better than producing a brilliantly prepared presentation giving full details of next year's production target when what was required was a five-year projection. So get the objective clear and then you are ready to follow Rudyard Kipling's advice and ask yourself "the Six Qs" (see over).

The careful answering of these questions is essential to good pre-planning, and the six basic questions give a structure that should avoid anything important being overlooked. Depending on the occasion, many additional headings to the ones given here may come to mind. Whilst the whole issue can be thought through at length before a major event, simply running though the Six Qs in your head either before or at a meeting can help bring to mind the right question to ask or the best slant to put on a statement.

This can also be a useful system to use when running a team-planning meeting, either by allocating one question to different individuals before group discussion or taking each in turn and accumulating a set of flip-charts with the various points displayed. This "open-cry" system is often an excellent way of attracting different or unusual thoughts and ideas which may prove to be a key success factor.

Even when it is not a team effort much can be gained by seeking out individual colleagues and asking their opinion – unless they are incredibly busy they will be pleased that you asked their advice.

If, however, it is just you alone preparing for an important speech, focusing on the Six Qs, once you are clear on the aim, will get you off to a well-structured start, and as the answers begin to appear any unnecessary fears or concerns may be allayed.

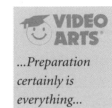

...Preparation certainly is everything...

Pre-planning

The six questions are the "Who?" "What?" "Why?" "When?" "Where?" and "How?" of perfect presentations. Finding out the answer to them before you even begin to think about what you are going to say is the essential first step to effective preparation. Take a look at them and think about them. Did you consider these points before you last pitched for some new business or asked your boss for a salary rise?

The six questions

1 WHO is attending?

- Who is my audience?
- Who are the individuals?
- What is their attitude –
  Supportive?
  Interested?
  Forced?
  Indifferent?
  Well informed?
  Disparate?
- How many people will there be?
- What are their circumstances?
- What is their level of knowledge?
- How much time are they prepared to give me?

2 WHAT do they want to hear?

- Why are they coming?
- What level of detail should I give?
- What do they already know?
- What do they need to know?
- What do they want from me?

3 WHY am I doing this?

- What is my/my boss's aim?
- What do I want to tell them?
- What is the main message?
- What is the purpose? Decide whether it is to:
  Teach or train = to learn
  In this case you need to focus on the three basics of explanation, demonstration, confirmation (by practice or test).
  Educate or inform = to understand
  In this case your listeners want to understand an issue and develop their current knowledge.
  Enthuse or persuade = to accept
  In this case you must "sell" an item, issue, process or policy

based on logical argument supported by solid fact.

Entertain = to amuse
In this case you need to create a clever and witty talk.

Most speeches will combine some or all of these objectives, but a clearly understood aim will affect the priority given to each of them. Check what the prime purpose is.

4 WHEN am I doing this?

- How much time does this give me for preparation and rehearsal?
- What other commitments have I got?

5 WHERE am I doing this?

- Is there a location map?
- Is there car parking?

- Is the room booked?
- Is it available to rehearse in?
- What is the size/shape of the room?
- What facilities are available (tea/coffee)?
- What aids systems are available?

6 HOW can I put my message across?

- What is the best way of achieving the aim:
  Lecture – formal or informal with good supporting material?
  Briefing – informal?
  Discussion – review or ask series of questions?
  Meeting with agenda?
  Book or paper?

The outline plan

Having asked and answered the Six Qs you are now ready for the next phase. This is to start planning the actual presentation. Some will wish to combine the Six Qs exercise with this, but in my view it is better to keep the pre-planning linked to a specific set of questions and separate from the free thinking of the speech planning stage.

In addition you may already realize that there are some specific areas of research you should do before the detailed planning can begin. This thinking stage gives the mind time to mull over possibilities and to store thoughts and ideas for later. It is also a time to talk to friends and colleagues to get their reaction to the "problem" and to give you some of their ideas. If you are in the (good) habit of keeping a notebook handy it will be useful to check your jottings before you start to plan in detail.

Those of us who have been confined to a "right-brain" upbringing will no doubt produce a list of points down the left-hand side of the page and then build on that. Those lucky enough to have been exposed to "mind-mapping" (Edward De Bono et al.) will let their thoughts develop more freely. The results from both approaches should be the same and are outlined opposite and over the page.

The objective at this stage is to get anything down in any order. You may do this as a brainstorm (use a flip-chart) or, if you have time, accrue your list over a couple of days as the ideas come to you.

Exercise

Have a look at the mind-map opposite and choose your own subject (rather than the "geo-mining" one given here). Develop the main points (your opening, the main issues, what you want to achieve, how you will close) and further sub-divide these into supporting points and issues, in the same way as branches on a tree sub-divide.

Once all the points you can readily think of are down, have a go at filling in the more traditional list over the page with the same information you have used on your mind map. Sometimes the free spirits of private enterprise find a structured approach to anything a bit of an anathema, but, if they leave out this vital part of the jigsaw of preparation, they run a real risk of failing to sell themselves as well as they should. So, try the structured approach first and then adapt it to suit your own circumstances once you are confident about the quality of your preparation.

Mind map for "Geo-mining"

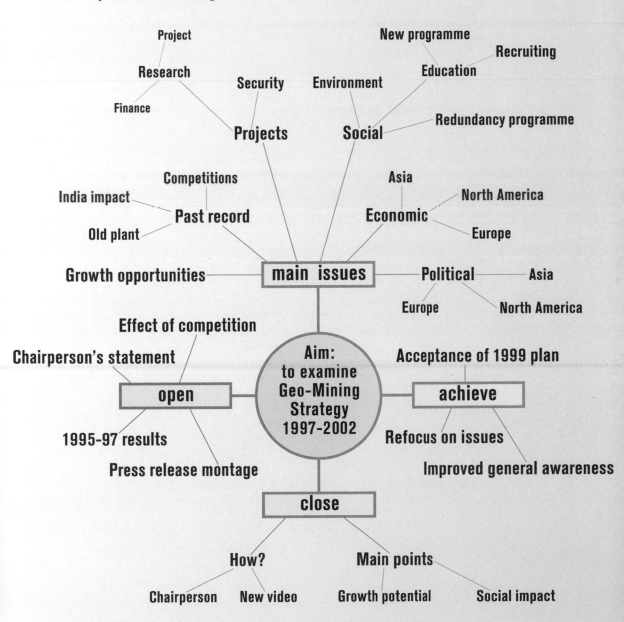

The outline plan

The structure

Aim - main message _____
_____

What do I want to achieve

1 _____

2 _____

3 _____

The title

_____

What major points or issues may be relevant

■ _____   ■ _____

■ _____   ■ _____

■ _____   ■ _____

■ _____   ■ _____

For each point or issue, note down 2-3 supporting points

1a _____

b _____

c _____

2a _____

b _____

c _____

3a _____
b _____
c _____

4a _____
b _____
c _____

5a _____
b _____
c _____

6a _____
b _____
c _____

7a _____
b _____
c _____

8a _____
b _____
c _____

List ideas for an exciting or memorable opening
1 _____
2 _____
3 _____

List ideas for a memorable ending
1 _____
2 _____
3 _____

The plan

The basics

Like most things in life, the perfect presentation has a beginning, a middle and an end. Each serves its own purpose, but sadly many of us miss the message by mixing them up. The basic structure is:

- The beginning – to excite and introduce.
  The middle – to inform and instruct.
  The end – to confirm and leave a lasting impression.
  Or:
- Say what you're going to say.
  Say it.
  Say it again.

This follows Harold Macmillan's advice of having only one to three good ideas and making the message stick by first "flagging" up an idea to get the attention of the listeners (introduction) and then waving it about (explanation) before firmly, by repetition, planting it in their minds (summary). This format ensures your message is clearly understood and remembered.

A garbled message, delivered as a plethora of points is memorable only for the confusion it creates. Therefore, the other essential basis of preparation is wrapped in the ever true mnemonic, "KISS" – keep it simple stupid!

From mind-map to structure

The best way to do this is to produce a final plan by combining the main points from your research in one structure plan. An example is given below for you to fill in.

Having got everything down in this way the next task is to prune and cut

Prospects for 1999

Aim: To brief managers on the company's prospects for 1999
Purpose: To gain commitment to the new structure
Location: Bridge Street Meeting Room. **Date:** 10:30am, 29 July. **Time:** 25 minutes

Introduction ➤	Main body ➤	Conclusion

out some aspects and issues. Look at the outline and think about:

- **What must the listener know and understand to achieve your aim?**
- **What should they know in addition?**
- **What could be added if there was time?**

The discipline of prioritizing your points into essential, important and useful is not always easy but failure to do so often leads to an overlong talk which fails to make the vital points.

Time plan

Having made the plan for the presentation you should be feeling more relaxed about the task. You know what you want to say and the main messages you want to put across. You have now reached another critical stage of preparation: planning the time you need for preparation and rehearsal. This needs careful thought to ensure that it doesn't clash with any of your other priorities and then estimate and allocate sufficient time so that you do not "fail to prepare – prepare to fail". Below is an example of the preparation plan:

Exercise

Take the subject of your mind-map/list or one of the ideas on p.55 and structure this into your outline plan for a 15-minute talk.

Exercise

Select a date two weeks ahead to "deliver" your speech and, using your current diary, make your time plan.

Prospects for 1999 time plan

- 31 July – Review
- 29 July – Deliver
- 28 July – Final rehearsal
- 27 July – Check all kit, location and admin arrangements
- 24 July – Second rehearsal
- 23 July – Collect and check visuals
- 20 July – Rehearse script and notes
- 18 July – Draft visual aids/prepare speaking notes
- 16 July – Revise script/final draft
- 10 July – Complete draft script
- 1 July – Complete outline

The start: preliminaries

Having completed your planning you are now ready to draft your script using the points and ideas you have identified and listed in your plan. You may prefer to go straight to the "meat" of your talk and sketch out the middle stage first. Getting this, longest section, sorted out first often helps to clarify things and makes the planning of the opening and closing segments easier to do. For ease of reference here, however, I will follow the logical sequence of beginning, middle and end.

The best mnemonic I have come across to help start a speech is:

I Ignite

N Need

T Title

R Range

O Objective

IGNITE

"By the time I have finished speaking to you today, 30 children will have been killed or seriously injured in a road accident."

"Ladies and gentlemen, this morning I am going to tell you how to add 20 percent to the value of your home."

NEED

"This terrible statistic can be radically reduced by three changes to the law – and this is something that every parent here will want to see actioned now."

"Your property is your most important asset and by the careful application of a few rules it is possible to preserve and enhance its value significantly. This is something every home owner should know about."

TITLE

"So this morning I want to spend some time telling you about Road Safety and the Law."

"The title of this talk is Land Rights and Property Values and it will cover the action you need to take to benefit from this legal but neglected opportunity."

RANGE

"I intend to talk for half an hour and cover the issues of lighting, education and police responsibility before showing you a film from Denmark, after which I would like to open the session for questions."

"During the next 40 minutes I am going to cover the historical and current legal situation and then project forward five years to show how taking action now will affect your estate. After a short break for questions I will then distribute the pack giving full details of the scheme and application forms."

OBJECTIVE

"At the end of this session I am sure you will wish to join the 1998 campaign to force the government to enact the law, changes we recommend in this session."

"My purpose in this is to give all the members of this Institution the opportunity to benefit from and take full advantage of their property rights."

This simple drill should be sufficient to interest the audience in the issue, give them a preview of how you will develop your ideas and detail the benefits they can gain.

This system works well if you and your subject have been introduced by the chairperson or organizer and, with the formalities over, you are free to make an immediate impact (ignition) on your audience. If you are not properly introduced, it is important to do so yourself. Often this is the best way anyway, as it gives your listeners a chance to settle down and "tune in" to your voice. It also allows you to get the

"feel" of the room and the audience by testing your RSVPP, enabling you to establish your authority. When you start speaking, your self-introduction should follow this sequence:

GREET

Take the opportunity to say "Good Morning" with a pleasant open smile that conveys the impression that you are pleased to be there.

IDENTIFY

Say who you are, where you are from and what you do.

QUALIFY

Give some indication of what you did, or are currently doing, which demonstrates your suitability/ qualification to speak on the subject.

TOPIC

Give the title of your talk.

TIME

Say how long the presentation will last.

SURPRISES

Give notice of any video, questionnaires or special effects to heighten anticipation.

QUESTIONS

Say when you would prefer to take questions.

The start: preliminaries

Exercise:

Look back at your plan. Work out the formal part of the introduction and practice giving it. Then try to work out one or two ideas for your ignition and try them. Finally select your ignition and practice giving the introduction and the ignition. The main thing this should achieve is to convince you that you now have an excellent system for settling both yourself and your audience before "hooking" them in with an exciting start. Now that you have "told them what you are going to tell them" you are ready to plan the important middle section and "tell them"!

For example:
- Good morning everybody.
- My name is John Collins and I am currently work as a business consultant specializing in Communication Skills.
- I have spent much of the last ten years in the City working on this and general management skills with graduates and executives. Before that I had a number of teaching and training jobs, which included Communication Skills Training at all levels within the Army.
- Today I would like to talk about and discuss the use and misuse of aids when making business presentations.
- As you know 40 minutes have been allotted to me and I will outline my ideas in 20 minutes...
- During which I will include a short film on how to make best use of your PC presentation package and show some good and horrid examples of slides...
- And after that I suggest we throw the forum open for your questions and comments.

NOW PAUSE – LOOK YOUR AUDIENCE IN THE EYE, AND THEN *CREATE IGNITION*.

IGNITION

After setting the scene, you are now ready to really begin your presentation. So, after a pause, the task is to get your listeners' full attention with a "hook" that ignites by either startling, intriguing, amusing, exciting or worrying them. You need an opening statement along the lines of the examples on page 52 related to your subject, which does one or all of these things. You can achieve this by:

- Asking a question.
- Reading a memorable quotation.
- Making a statement which arouses curiosity, surprise or intrigue.
- Telling a short story which illustrates your theme.
- Outlining the benefits which could be achieved if...
- Using an arresting slide or OHP.

Your opening should be short, sharp and to the point. The days of softening the listeners with an unrelated joke are out. Related ones are in, provided you are confident the audience will like it, and you can deliver the punch line without a hitch!

When preparing a talk do not spend too much time initially trying to think of your ignition. It is often better to plan the formal stage of the talk first and begin by working on the main part. The inspiration for an exciting opening may come to you at any time!

The middle

Continue to follow Macmillan's advice and focus on two to three main themes for your subject. For example:

■ Social – Economic – Political.
■ Past – Present – Future.
■ Evasion – Avoidance – Planning.
■ Current System – Proposed System.

Each theme becomes a mini-presentation of its own and can be amplified by one or two supporting points, which enable you to maintain interest while making a logical progression through the story or argument.

Your concern now is how to maintain the undivided attention of your listeners. If you accept the research that states that we remember only:

10 % of what we read
20 % of what we hear
30 % of what we see
50 % of what we see and hear

It is clear that you have a battle on your hands! However, I do not believe these figures relate to a business or professional presentation. Professionals are paid to derive benefit from any business contact and they listen carefully to what is said. It also helps if the visuals work well.

These figures do not include "seeing" the speaker and, in my view, they should. As explained later, the best visual aid is you, and if your speech and body language create the right atmosphere for your audience, they will remember your message. Exciting visuals help to make an impact, but only if they are mixed and matched by an interesting speaker. Those who subject their audience to an unrelenting stream of slides seem to forget this.

To maintain interest focus on the following:

■ Delivery will continue to be a vital ingredient throughout your talk. Keep the RSVPP going (see p29).
■ Make the argument easy to follow by developing it in logical steps and keeping to the point.
■ Give relevant examples or tell anecdotes to illustrate your points. Everyone likes a story.
■ Where possible personalize your story with your own experience, practice and knowledge. This underlines your position as an authority on the subject and, by drawing support and sometimes sympathy from your audience, helps maintain your rapport with them during the presentation. Personalizing also means creating a more informal and relaxed style by using "I", "we" and "us" and less of the "you" or, worse still, "one".

The middle

Because the audience have not seen or read your script and have little idea of what is coming next you must help them to follow your thoughts. This can be achieved by getting the pace right, pausing to give time for words (and diagrams) to make an impact and be understood, and giving a helpful signpost when you are about to move on to the next theme.

Sometimes using questions to keep your audience involved can be useful. Even rhetorical questions can help maintain interest. Ask them your question before you explain a point, if your aim is to involve the group; ask it after your explanation, if you wish to confirm their understanding.

■ Appropriate language.
For your listeners to understand your talk you must pitch the language at the right level. Sound condescending and you are lost; sound over-complicated and you will begin to see the lights going out! Getting the level right is not easy, particularly as an audience often covers a spectrum of knowledge and interest.

A briefing to a client and his adviser poses another dilemma as the adviser may well have a sophisticated understanding of the subject while the client, the ultimate decision-maker, probably does not. It takes experience to learn which parts of a speech to pitch at whom to avoid offending both!

If in doubt, always pitch to the highest common denominator not the lowest.

■ Keep to the facts, simply said, and be specific in your focus on the subject and themes.

■ Use short, sharp sentences, finishing with a pause long enough to allow you to engage in eye contact and ask the silent question "Did you get that?"

■ They will get it if you can dramatize your point with a good story or example or an arresting statement delivered with vigour and conviction.
It doesn't matter whether you are describing the merits of a merger or a hamburger, unless your words and tone are enthusiastic and committed you will lose any rapport with your listeners.

■ Your audience will also get lost if you fail to link and signpost the development of your argument. Remember that they are hearing your beautifully prepared and rehearsed presentation for the first time. Unlike you, they do not know what is coming next. So they need signposts to tell them that one theme is finished and another is about to begin linking one subject to the next. For example: "For the last few minutes we have looked at the social implications of the new wage structure (saying it again). Now let's look at the process we must put into place to get this to work" (say what you're going to say).

Think of each of your two to three chosen themes as a mini-presentation with its own PREP or, if you prefer, its own SPEC (p32): Spark – Purpose – Example – Conclusion.

The conclusion

And so we reach the final and vital part of your presentation – the ending and how to make sure that your audience remember your message. To ensure that the message is the climax, it is best to follow a set pattern.

First, lead into the conclusion at the end of your last main theme. Let the audience know you have reached that point, not by saying "in conclusion", but with something like, "with that point let us briefly recap on the main issues we have looked at. They were…"

Now ask for and answer questions (for details see Chapter 6).

Thank your audience for listening and being involved. Make any necessary administrative announcements, collect handouts or completed questionnaires.

NOW make your final closing statement or comment in such a way that your message is driven home in an unforgettable climax.

This could be:
- A call to action.
- A look to the future.
- A question.
- A commitment.
- A statement.

It should be delivered with firmness and conviction directly to the audience without reference to notes.

Keep looking at your audience, smile and either sit down or step back. There is no need to say anything further, certainly not "thank you" again. Let the message sink in and be the last thing remembered from your speech.

The conclusion: an example
"That story neatly brings me to the point where I would like to briefly review the issues and open up for question and comment.

"We have seen that whilst there are advantages to the present system of salary review, there are many problems which make it unfair to our junior staff.

"We have had a close look at the proposed system and as the film from our American partners showed, with allowance made for the UK scene, it will be possible and extremely worthwhile in the long run to introduce the new system next year.

"Now would anyone care to comment or ask any questions? *(After questions)*

"Well that has been a useful session and thank you for treating me so gently.

"I think I should just remind you that there is a pack detailing the proposals for your collection on the way out and of course you know that the Managing Director will be briefing each department in turn starting on Wednesday."

Getting feedback

The final steps

There are two remaining issues to think about: the question and answer session and the aids you want to use. These are important matters and merit their own chapters. When you have read them, you may wish to complete your presentation preparation, test your skill on a new subject or, better still, work on an actual brief you have to deliver.

The review

After the talk is finished you will undoubtedly have a sense of satisfaction probably followed by a feeling of anti-climax. There is, however, still one more important thing to do, particularly if you want to continue to improve your skills. This, of course, is to get some feedback on your performance. It can be done informally by phoning (after a day or so) a few individuals who were in the audience.

Alternatively you can ask a few friends, colleagues or other participants who are prepared to help to fill in a simple questionnaire. This questionnaire is not the same as the very detailed one you used at rehearsals, because you should not expect members of your audience to focus in detail on your presentation skills when they are supposed to be taking in your message. Compare all the comments to see what went well and what could be improved, and put them in your Presentations File to refer to before you start work on your next speaking task.

Feedback can also be obtained formally, especially at a major event where the organizers may well issue forms to all the delegates asking for their comments on both the content and delivery of your speech. Make sure that you are given a copy of this.

Examples of both types of review are given opposite and over the page.

| Feedback: | The New Pay Structure | | Date |

Thank you for listening to my brief today. If you can spare the time I would be grateful for any comments you may have on both the content and the delivery. This will be helpful both to me and those forced to listen to me in the future!

Would you please grade on a scale of 1–10 (10 = Useless, 1 = brilliant)

- Did I make the aim of the talk clear?
- Did I appear to know what I was talking about?
- Was the talk structured, logical and easy to follow?
- Was the subject matter interesting?
- Was it put across in an interesting manner?
- Did you feel the audience was involved?
- Was my voice clear?
- Were the aids helpful?
- Did the question and answer session meet your needs?
- Did I appear confident?

Have you any suggestions to help me improve in the future?

Many thanks

Getting feedback

Rehearsal questionnaire

Speaker	Excellent	Average	Unsatisfactory	Subject	Date
Speech outline					
Skill in establishing rapport				**Comments**	
Personal appearance					
Evidence of confidence					
Suitability of material					
Eye contact					
Facial expression					
Body posture					
Use of gesture					
Use of voice				**Comments**	
Rhythm					
Speed					
Volume					
Pitch					
Pause					
Use of gesture					
Evidence of Preparation				**Comments**	
Knowledge of Subject					
Organization					
Links between sections					
Overall unity of speech					
Use of aids					
Delivery				**Comments**	
Introduction - effectiveness					
Main body - effectiveness					
Conclusion - effectiveness					
Audience interest				**Comments**	
Participation					
Questions - to and from					

Making it happen

This long chapter has concentrated on one of the two basic essentials of effective presentation, preparation, and has shown how, by logically developing your thoughts and ideas in a structured manner, all the aspects that should lead to success will be covered.

However, I know many busy executives just do not have the time to prepare effectively and the presentations will continue to be last minute affairs. As there are so many other factors which may determine whether or not a pitch or briefing was won or lost, it is unlikely that the presentation itself will be blamed for any perceived failure.

Whatever the outcome, there will have been areas for improvement, and perhaps the best way to get this recognized, is to force a review after the session. This could be the first step in acknowledging that there are areas that can be improved by accepting the need for adequate preparation and rehearsal.

It is not difficult to get executives to acknowledge the logic of the case for structured preparation and even to issue the instructions insisting that in future it must be actioned. The need, then, is to ensure that this continues as a basic business practice. Needless to say, this will not happen unless there is sustained support and attention from the senior managers.

Summary

To ensure that your preparation lays the foundation to successful delivery on the day:
- Be clear on the aim.
- Ask the six Qs.
- Brainstorm your structure with a list or mind-map.
- Decide what your audience must, should and could know.
- Draft a structured plan with a beginning, a middle and an end.
- Say what you're going to say, and say it and say it again.
- We remember 50 percent of what we see and hear, but you are the best visual aid.
- Make a realistic preparation plan.
- Ignite your audience.
- Develop your talk in logical stages.
- Signpost each stage.
- Give examples, stories, anecdotes – personalize where possible.
- Make your ending memorable.
- KISS and KISS again.
- Review and make notes for the future in your Presentations File.

5

The use of visual aids
Design
Equipment

A picture is worth a thousand words

The most important visual aid is you!

Are your visuals really necessary?

Uses and abuses of visuals

Properly used visual aids can add enormous impact and effect to your presentation. They can illustrate and demonstrate points, processes and ideas that are too difficult to explain verbally. They can provide interest and variety, create the right atmosphere and, most important of all, can have a lasting impression which will outlive the words that accompanied them. When badly used, however, they will produce a result quite different from what you hoped would be a spectacular display.

Sadly the ease with which transparencies and computer graphics can now be produced frequently results in them being anything but an aid to either the speaker or the audience. You will perhaps recall the research quoted in Chapter 4 which stated that we remember:

10% of what we read

20 % of what we hear

30 % of what we see

50 % of what we see and hear

This is only true, though, if what is said is coordinated with what is seen and one aspect complements the other. To achieve this, make sure that the concept, design and construction of your visual aids are an integral part of your preparation, and their delivery an integral part of your rehearsal. To do this properly requires a basic understanding of visual aids, their proper uses and purpose.

Proper uses

A visual aid has one of three purposes. These are:

■ To make, explain or identify a point or process.
■ To emphasize, clarify or reinforce a point or process.
■ To remind, summarize or review a point or process.

All three help the listener to remember key points, support your case and reinforce what you say. They increase rapport, create rhythm, inject variety, simplify the complicated and add interest to the story. How you use the aid and its design depend on its purpose, but whatever the purpose two simple rules always apply:

■ KISS (see p50): The visual message that is short, simple and stark makes a memorable impact.
■ REHEARSE: To complement the flow of delivery the equipment must work impeccably and the visuals create the impression they were designed for. This cannot be achieved without really effective rehearsal.

Abuses of visuals:

Design

■ **Long lists stating everything the speaker is going to say.**
The listeners will be reading at a far greater speed than the presenter will be speaking. Individuals will not listen to what is being said.

■ **Unnecessary pictures.**
A few informative, well-prepared slides will be enough.

■ **Over-complicated charts, graphs and diagrams, too small to be read.**
Detailed graphs and drawings must be designed for the screen, so the message is easily understood.

■ **Designed to impress but not to support/aid the speaker.**
Computer graphics may look good, but not add to the message.

■ **No pictures when one is needed.**
This is the other end of the scale, when a picture is needed to explain a complicated point.

■ **Using only words and no images.**
A picture or an image instead of a word description will make a more lasting impact.

Delivery

■ **No time given to the audience to understand the images used.**
The audience is seeing the image for the first time. They need time to absorb the information.

■ **Images left on screen when the speaker is on the next point.**
A major irritation for the listener is "out of date" information remains on screen and confuses the point being made.

■ **Speaker talks to the visual and ignores the listener.**
After checking to see that the correct slide is on the screen, the presenter talks to his pictures and seemingly forgets all eye contact with his audience.

■ **Speaker ignores the visual.**
For some reason, a picture appears, but to the audience there is no apparent connection between it and what is being said.

■ **Information read word for word.**
The audience is able to read for itself. The speaker does not have to read every word out loud.

Design: pictures and words

Pictures and word slides

Whenever possible, a picture, rather than words, should be used to illustrate a point. The impact of a picture, expanded by spoken (not written) words is greater than a mere list of words.

When you use words, show them in an interesting manner. Compare the effectiveness of the images illustrating "delivery" in the following examples. Clearly, the bottom one is far better than the plain list on the left.

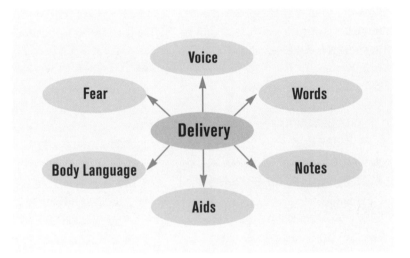

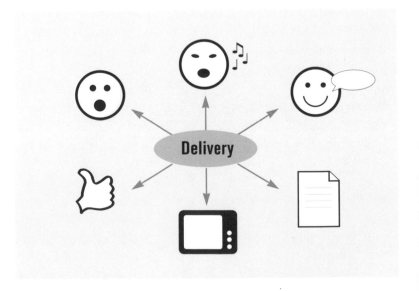

Design: graphs

Visuals are a combination of pictures, words or graphs (charts) and they have different uses and applications. A look at any report and accounts from a large company that is trying to be user-friendly towards its shareholders usually demonstrates a careful use of them all. We should do the same with our own presentations.

The excellent Video Arts booklet on choosing and using charts identifies seven types of chart or graph, all of which aim to demonstrate the comparisons between different data or facts. The skill is in deciding which type of graph (pie, column, bar, curve, etc) will be best suited to illustrate the comparisons, shown below. The seven basic types of graph are overleaf.

Types of data comparison

- **Component Comparison** – Shows the relative size of a component within a total, that is its contribution, share, percentage of a total.
- **Item Comparison** – Shows a ranking of items comparing either their size, value or quantity.
- **Time Series Comparison** – Shows how the quantity of an item varies over time.
- **Frequency Distribution Comparison** – Shows the quantity of an item in each of several amount categories of progressive size or rank.
- **Co-relationship Comparison** – Shows how variation in one respect relates to variation in another.

Design: graphs

■ **Pie Charts:** The circle is best suited to show the relative sizes or share of a particular aspect, for instance different costs, percentage of products required, amount spent by each department. This works well if there aren't too many segments. It is also easier on the eye if the segments start at twelve o'clock.

As the examples below show, the pie chart gives an instant accurate picture of relative size, either using a single pie, omitting a segment or by using more than one pie.

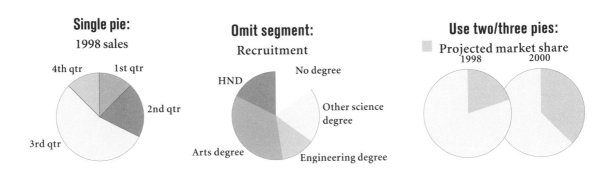

Single pie:
1998 sales

4th qtr 1st qtr
3rd qtr 2nd qtr

Omit segment:
Recruitment

HND No degree
Arts degree Other science degree
Engineering degree

Use two/three pies:
■ Projected market share
1998   2000

■ **Bar Charts:** These are useful for showing how items compare, for instance, individual brands' performances or anything where there is a need to show what various groups have achieved over a set time scale. The graph can be either vertical or horizontal, but generally the horizontal is best as there is more space to write in the item headings.

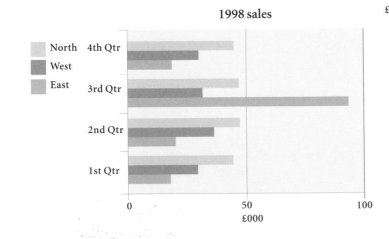

1998 sales

North
West
East

4th Qtr
3rd Qtr
2nd Qtr
1st Qtr

0   50   100
£000

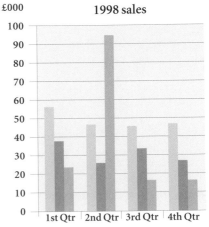

£000   1998 sales

100
90
80
70
60
50
40
30
20
10
0
    1st Qtr   2nd Qtr   3rd Qtr   4th Qtr

■ **Column Graphs:** These are usually used to show how the quantity of an item has varied over time, for instance annual growth/decline, climate variation, salary change.

They can cover any unit of time, enabling the viewer to immediately see the fluctuations and changes over a historical period and indicate future trends.

Salary costs 1986 – 96

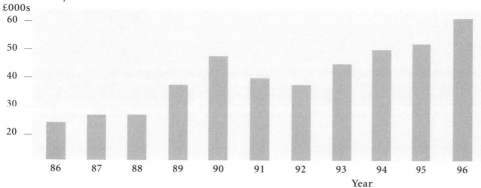

■ **Step Graphs:** These are column graphs, but with no space shown between the columns. They are particularly useful for showing information that changes abruptly at irregular intervals.

■ **Curve Graphs:** These are similar to column graphs but are used when there are a large number of points to be plotted. The graph emphasizes flow and change, for instance entries per month or client contacts.

Salary costs 1986 – 96

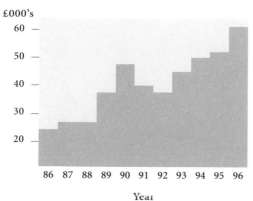

Employee – Age spread

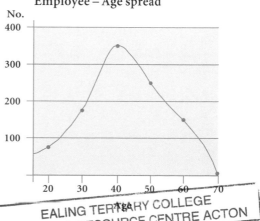

Design: graphs

Remember the need to keep the slide simple. Often this can be achieved by using a sequence of slides to build up a picture, explaining the development as you go along and even taking questions at each stage to confirm that it is understood before moving on to the next one.

A careful and conservative use of colour is also important. Careful in that the colour used for the letters must differ sufficiently from that used for the background to make them stand out and be easy to read. Conservative in that only two or three colours should be used. More than that and the image loses its sharpness and is less easy to remember.

■ **Surface Graphs:** Shading in the area formed by a curve graph (see previous page) helps to highlight quantities and emphasizes the sweep of the curve. It also emphasizes the peak of the curve, and is generally clearer and visually more effective than the more basic curve graph.

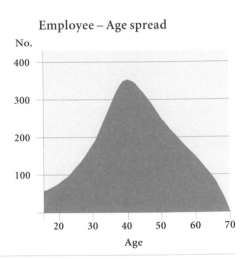

Employee – Age spread

■ **Scattergrams:** Though rarely used these can be an effective way of pinpointing individual results and demonstrating the general trend and density of the norm, especially where hundreds of results are involved.

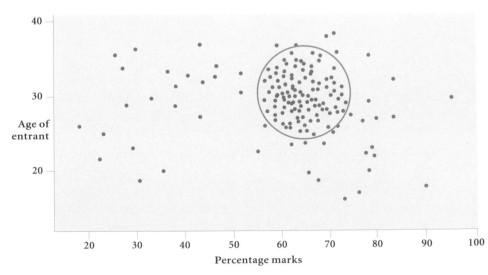

Exam results – Age correlation

The equipment

The main types of visual used today are computer graphics, the transparency, the slide and the flip-chart. Some schools still use the chalk-board, the white-board or even the flannel-board, but as the use and design of these is similar to the flip-chart I will not include them here. Videos can also be used to add a further dimension to presentations. Each of the main types has advantages and disadvantages for the presenter. Let's look at each in turn:

The computer

Computer-generated graphics are fast becoming the mainstay of the business presentation and with the right equipment can be used for any size group. The computer-literate presenter, preparing a presentation, now has at his fingertips the means of creating, amending, copying, inserting, changing the order and retrieving almost any type of image. He can also alter and fine tune, as appropriate, at the initial rehearsals.

It is this very abundance of opportunity that can also be the cause of disappointment, if you don't know how to use the technology properly. If the wrong buttons are pressed the show can quickly become a shambles, and if you have to send for an IT technician to sort it out, your performance will be a total disaster!

Today's computer-literate young executives do not have these problems. The mistake they make is being over-enthused with the technology which produces a high-tech display but fails to keep the message simple and detracts from their own performance.

It is important to insist that the computer graphics can be seen in normal room light. Those in search of perfect picture clarity (the technicians) will attempt to persuade the presenter to speak in a darkened room. Agree to this and you surrender your eye contact and rapport with your audience. If your aim is that the visuals should support what you are saying, insist on you and your audience being able to see each other. Of course, if it is a short video clip, it is in order for the lights to go down while everyone listens to the film commentary and not to you. When the lights go up again, you are there and can regain control.

However, with that warning in mind, there is no doubt that computer graphics are becoming the most effective method of visual aid, and any business presenter needs to master its techniques. The system for showing the visual is the same as for the transparency discussed below, except that you do not have to handle anything other than your mouse or keyboard, which should simplify and streamline the whole operation.

Transparencies

The overhead projector is still the presenter's workhorse. Transparencies are cheap to make and can be added to while you talk. They too can be easily produced on the computer and printed as an OHP in either black and white (and then coloured using non-permanent colour pens if required) or produced on a colour copier.

They are somewhat clumsy to use and in light of the more hi-tech equipment now available are beginning to feel, look and sound old-fashioned (they are noisy!). Used properly, however, they create an informal atmosphere and work well with no threat to the daylight! Some simple rules governing how they should and should not be used are given below.

They may all seem obvious and too long-winded a process, but ignoring any of these points almost certainly means that you end up ignoring your listeners, which, as we have already seen, is a cardinal sin.

Before you start

- Design with simplicity in mind. If you must use words then no more than seven lines and six words per line.

Check

- The focus.
- That the picture fills 75 percent of the screen.
- That everyone can see the screen (the machine itself can often block the view).
- That your OHPs are in order and numbered and you know where you will put them when used.
- That the machine is switched off.

When you start

- Pause – stop talking. Pick up your first OHP and place it squarely on the frame.
- Switch on the machine.
- Pause – give people time to read the OHP.
- Face the audience not the screen.
- Explain your points.
- Use a pointer on the OHP – not the screen.

When finished

- Stop talking.
- Switch off the machine.
- Remove the OHP.
- Place your next OHP on the frame.
- Face the audience.
- Continue talking.

Repeat the sequence for the next OHP.

Slides

Until recently, slides were probably the most popular aid for presenters, particularly to large audiences. They are professionally produced and look very good. However, computer-based aids are quite rightly fast taking over as the prime option. The main advantage of the slide is the clarity of the picture and, if this is important, the slide is the best medium and should be used.

To achieve this clarity you will almost certainly have to show the slide in a darkened room. This is my main objection to using them because darkness results in the most important visual aid (YOU) being sidelined!

Therefore slides are best used as a sequence of pictures at a particular point of the briefing so that you remain in visual contact for the majority of the time and are not disrupting proceedings by constantly plunging the room into darkness.

If absolute clarity of picture is not required, the slide can be shown with the lights dimmed rather than off. This compromise works well, allowing you still to be seen – even if the technicians don't approve!

...Slides can save time, they can create interest, add variety and provide impact...

Before you start
- Design with simplicity in mind. If you must use words then no more than seven lines and six words per line.
- Mark each slide with a sequence number so they are in order.
- Mark each slide at the top-right corner so that you are certain to load each one correctly.
- Check to see that they are in the right order, the right way up, and focused.
- Insert blanks between each slide.
- Don't drop the box.

When you start
- Lights down – if you must.
- Switch on.
- Recheck focus.
- Pause – give the audience time to read and understand.
- Explain your slide.
- Face the audience except when indicating something on the screen.
- Use a torchlight or a pointer.

When finished
- Lights up (if you had to have them down).
- Don't leave the slide on; move to blank or to the next slide.
- If there is a long gap between slides, switch off.

The flip-chart

Flip-charts are an excellent aid for teaching and training small groups and for informal briefings or brainstorming sessions. They can be prepared before a lecture and added to during it. They are particularly useful for gaining audience involvement by calling for their ideas and suggestions while "building" a chart or headings list. Pages can be torn from the pad and stuck to the wall for reference. Here are a few points to remember:

Before you start
- Sketch your slide lightly in pencil so that only you can see. Be sure you get the spacing and letter size right.
- Make sure the letters are large enough to read easily – 6 cms for headings and no less than 3 cms for anything else.
- Use thick edge of felt-tip for letters, the reverse for lines.
- Not more than three colours – strong, bold ones are best.
- Plenty of white space.
- Lightly pencil in any memory joggers down the side where only you can see them.
- Tab a corner with a one-word title so that you can see which flip you want when you want it.
- Make sure you have good-quality pens available at the session.
- Decide where to position the chart stand so that it does not dominate your space but can be used easily and moved if necessary.

When you start
- Don't talk and write at the same time.
- Introduce – pause – display – pause – talk/invite comment.
- Stand beside, not in front of, the chart when you are writing on it and when you are talking.

When you have finished
- Turn to blank flip. Do not leave the last theme on display when you introduce the next.
- Stop fiddling with the marker and put it back on the rack!

Video

Any presentation can be enlivened by a relevant video clip and there are also many excellent full-length video films to assist specific training sessions. Specially commissioned films, if the funds are available, can make an enormous impact (a good one if the film is well made and the exact opposite if it is not!). Points to remember:

VIDEO ARTS

...If you're going to use technology, use it to support your arguments, not to replace them...

Before you start

- Preview the video and make sure its message and style coincide with your own.
- Make sure you and the video tell the same story. Otherwise amend your script if you have to, or ditch the video.
- Find out how the equipment works (including remote controls).
- Check that the screen is large enough to be easily seen. If not, use monitor screens around the room.
- Wind the video to the start of the tape or to the beginning of the piece you wish to show; check that you have got it right.

When you start

- Introduce the video (unless you are seeking a dramatic "ignition").
- Lights down.
- If you wish to comment on a point, stop the video. Make your point and then restart. Do not try to talk over the narrator. This is very irritating for the listener!
- Do not interrupt too often by stopping and starting the tape.

When finished

- Stop the machine. Do not rewind.
- If you have a second video to show, eject the used one and insert the new one.
- Lights up!

Handouts

With few exceptions the rule is: "Do not hand out handouts before a presentation." If you do, you will almost certainly lose some of your audience, as they will happily let their mind wander through your handout way in advance of what you are saying. They will focus on the issues which interest then but them rob you of the opportunity to put the case in the way you wish. Worse still, if your voice is just a background to the reading of your supposed listeners, then you have little chance of developing a rapport or of impressing them with your personal style and integrity.

Nevertheless it is common practice in business to issue a handout before the presentation. It is also sadly common for the audience to be seen reading or flicking through the handout in advance while the poor, usually junior, executive gradually loses confidence and authority as he realizes that no one is listening to him.

Whenever possible hold the handout to the end. If you must, circulate individual handouts only as they are needed. This will allow you to maintain some control and to keep in contact with your listeners for most of the time.

For some business presentations, the decision will be made that there will be no "slide show" or formal briefing, but a working meeting to "go through the figures". This will be because client and advisor know each other so well that the need of being convinced on issues of integrity, experience and skill is well past. For this meeting, the style is intended to be intimate, relaxed and informal, to allow the clients to focus entirely on the facts and their interpretation.

To achieve this, a detailed handout is produced which is systematically worked through during the meeting with heads buried in the figures for most of the session.

The success of this session will depend, in the main, on the quality of the briefing material, and the development of effective discussion between those involved. The need for careful preparation and rehearsed delivery remain.

Exercise

Draft some OHPs to support your presentation: Try different ways to convey your message. Select the best. Now think what changes you would make if you used a slide or a flip-chart instead. Decide which would be best for this assignment.

You!

Despite all of the previous material, remember that the most important visual aid is you. However brilliant the script and the aids it is your style, personality and enthusiasm which will create the lasting impression.

As for dress, apart from the normal nanny advice of combed hair, clean faces and so on, the clearest advice is to dress in the same style as your audience. (If you take your jacket off, invite the audience to do the same).

Men should avoid short socks that show the ankle and women short skirts that show the knee when sitting on a platform. Both should avoid distracting jewellery!

There are books that go into greater detail on the subject of appearance, but I prefer to re-state that you should dress to suit the occasion and the audience, and that in addition to style and body language, there is some truth in the old adage – whatever you say, your clothes say more!

Summary

Visual aids should be a valuable addition to any presentation. But remember the following:
- YOU are the most important visual aid; don't let the visual usurp you!
- Avoid "Death by Slide/OHP" – too few is better than too many.
- Practise using the equipment before you present.
- Don't talk and operate the equipment or write at the same time.
- Write neatly.
- Don't talk to the screen.
- Use only two or three colours.
- Pause – put on – pause – talk – pause – stop talking – switch off – replace.

Use your slide to:
- Introduce.
- Make a point – emphasize – reinforce.
- Summarize.
- And above all rehearse, rehearse and dress rehearse using the visuals exactly as you intend to do on "the day".

6

The question and answer session
Staying in control
Other aspects of the session

Question and answer checklist

Difficult questioners

Asking the audience questions

The question and answer session

Having thought about the questions, prepare and rehearse short specific replies. PREP can be an excellent format for question answering.

If you hit on an important issue that you would like to see raised but do not have time to deal with in the main part of your speech, then flag it up as a rhetorical question and mention during your talk that "perhaps someone would like to pursue that point in the question session". Or, alternatively, "plant" the question with one of your colleagues. Planting one or two questions can also be a useful way of ensuring that the question session gets off to a good start.

The penultimate part of your presentation is taking questions from the audience. This is always an important part of the session in any context, but in business it is crucial and is the deciding factor in the success or failure of your presentation.

Despite its importance, the question session is often the least prepared and worst presented. It needn't be, as the application of the basic speaking skills plus some careful preparation are all that is required to make it a success.

The purpose

For the listeners the purpose of asking questions is to raise matters which they want to clarify, expand, challenge or test. Their intention should be to contribute to the proceedings. (It usually is, but sometimes their hidden agenda is to demonstrate their own expertise and belittle the speaker.)

For the speaker, the purpose is to close any gap of understanding on any aspect of your talk the questioner (and probably other members of the audience) may have. In addition, it is an opportunity to impress on the audience that you really know your subject. If you handle the questions with grace and skill it adds to the good rapport you have already established with the listeners. So let's think about the preparation and delivery in turn and then practise them.

Preparation

When you invite questions you are for the first time in your presentation giving up control to members of your audience. Your aim must be to regain that control as quickly as possible and retain it until you surrender it to the next questioner. The best preparation is to spend time beforehand working out the questions that your audience ought to ask and especially those you would prefer they did not! You can also ask your colleagues at the first rehearsal to think particularly hard about this and suggest some likely questions to you. Then draft and rehearse your answers.

These possible questions and answers should be added to your presentation cards or to the bottom of your A4 notes. Use them to refresh your mind before you speak, but do not refer to them during the question session when your answers must appear to be spontaneous. However, indicating that you were anticipating a question on those lines is fair enough. If you also have a "spare" slide which you prepared in case the question came up, then you will probably earn bonus points from your audience!

Handling questions and answers

It is important to invite questions in an encouraging and pleasant manner. So face the audience with a confident smile and say something like:

"Well, during the last twenty minutes I have covered the three main reasons why I believe we should support this proposal. And before I go any further (that is, summarize and end with impact) I think this would be a good time to answer any points or queries you may have."

If you are unlucky enough not to get a question and the silence becomes too excruciating because either your chairperson has failed one of their main duties (of always being ready to ask a question if no-one else does) or your "plant" has flunked it, you can start the ball rolling by returning to one of the rhetorical questions you asked during your talk. Try saying:

"Well, to get things going perhaps I should comment briefly on the question I raised but did not answer when talking about quotas. The point here is..."

If you do not get a second question after that you have no alternative but to move to the end and climax of the talk. Under no circumstances invite or beg for questions again!

Usually, however, audiences do ask questions and the suggested sequence for dealing with them is outlined below. While it appears somewhat laborious when you read it, your mind will flash through the process, as the action is, of course, taking place at speed. Follow these steps:

Listen

Listening carefully is a most important and often neglected skill. Do not interrupt the questioner to give an answer before you have really understood what – and more importantly why – you are being asked a question. Focus hard and concentrate.

Let your body language show that you are listening, by maintaining eye contact with the questioner throughout. (If it is a long question, it is better to also briefly sweep the audience also to gauge their reaction to it.) Leaning slightly forward, head to one side, or perhaps nodding, conveys the message that you are listening. Giving the odd grunt of acknowledgement from time to time can help, too.

Acknowledge

Acknowledge the question by saying "thank you". But take care not to patronize the questioner by complimenting him or her on an "excellent", or "well thought out" question unless you really mean it!

Handling questions and answers

Pause

Pause after the question to show that it is valid and requires some thought. This prevents you from rattling off an unconsidered reply that misses the point or is poorly constructed. During the pause:

DECIDE what the questioner wants. Is it:

- More information about what you have said?
- To clarify an issue you have raised?
- To express doubt about your argument?
- To express their own views and ideas?

Decide

What type of question you have been asked. Is it:

- Simple? Give a short, concise answer.
- Complicated? Relate to your main themes: clarify with a story or an example; summarize your reply.
- One you do not know the answer to? Say you will find out and get back to them (and make sure you do!). Give a contact who will know the answer. Ask if anyone in the audience can help. Move on by looking elsewhere and inviting the next question.
- Loaded (a question which is prejudiced, self-opinionated and self-seeking and usually more of a long-winded speech than a question)? Don't answer but invite the questioner to raise it with you afterwards (they won't) and then look elsewhere for the next question.
- Rambling? Ask the speaker what the actual question is and then either answer it very briefly, move on, or invite them to see you after.
- A repeated point? If the question repeats a point you have already made, say so. Refer briefly to what you said and, if it suits you, give a further example; if not, move on.
- Irrelevant? Acknowledge that it is interesting, or important, but not part of your subject today though it could be worth discussing afterwards; move on.
- A comment not a question? If the questioner is agreeing with you, just say thank you and move on. If the questioner is adding supporting material to your case, accept and acknowledge the point with thanks and move on.
- An objection? Either accept the point and agree to differ, repeat and re-explain your own argument, or offer some compromise between the two views.
- Multiple (a series of questions)? Say you can't answer them all; take the most interesting or relevant one; move on.

- One that highlights a serious weakness in your argument? Accept that this is an issue and explain what is or will be done to overcome it; don't fudge, maintain rapport by being honest and fair.

Remember

When you are asked a question, your mind whirrs into action to identify its nature and intent. If you think the rest of the audience is not clear on the question, or, worse still, you yourself are not sure, then either repeat or paraphrase it. This gives credit to the questioner while allowing you more thinking time. You are then back in control and ready to give a clear reply which enhances your reputation and rapport with your audience.

Answer

Keep your answers short, concise and to the point. Whenever possible link them to your earlier comments but, if appropriate, give new examples or anecdotes. It is important to retain a confident style during this session and to use RSVPP (p29) effectively. PREP (32), too, can be helpful. It is vital to inject enthusiasm into your voice and make it clear that this is an important part of the proceedings.

Work out a system for giving your answers so that you can focus fully on what you are going to say. For example:

Question: Do you think the English football team fixtures should be on terrestrial or satellite television?
Answer: I think they should be on terrestrial TV. *(Position)*
With a satellite TV monopoly, very few young people are going to be able to watch the matches live. *(Reason)*
I am sure that very few people bothered to watch the replay of yesterday's match twelve hours after the highlights were shown on the news. *(Example)*
So, yes, I do think these national events should be made available to all. *(Restate position)*

Confirm

Check with the questioner that you have answered his query.

A question from you, such as: "*Does that help/answer/clarify your question?*", confirms that you have closed the information gap, maintains your control and gives you the opportunity to say more. Invite further discussion afterwards or move on to your next point.

Move on

Don't linger over your answers, move on to the next question at a brisk, business-like pace.

The next step is to be ready to decide on the right moment to stop the question and answer session and enter the last part of your presentation.

Other aspects of questions and answers

Difficult Questioners

Every presenter dreads the difficult or confrontational question which is designed to destroy the impact of your message. Dealing with these rare occasions is an important skill and it is worth remembering a few ground rules. When dealing with the problem questioner:

- Try to win him over to your side.
- Your task is to deal with the question in a cool, calm fashion and at all costs avoid loss of temper.

Your method is to:

- Remain calm as the question unfolds.
- Use your preparation and knowledge of the subject to formulate you answer.
- Avoid personalizing the situation with personal abuse or sarcasm.
- Take the question and questioner seriously.
- Try to identify areas of agreement where you can establish common ground.
- If appropriate and necessary accept and take note of the criticism.
- Be prepared to apologise or admit to your error.

And then:

- React gently.
- Use quiet and non-aggressive language and tone.
- Be gracious and avoid flattening the questioner.
- Keep or return to the main issues.

- Be prepared to acknowledge the point but to deal with it later.
- Use controlled anger to accept the point.

If, however, all else fails and no-one has come to your rescue, be firm and sharp and move on!

Asking questions

During a speech or presentation you may wish to ask a question or start a discussion with your audience. It is worth remembering that the way you ask a question will dictate the sort of answer you will get. Questions can be:

- Rhetorical: not a real question, as it requires no answer! A useful play for presenters but should be used sparingly.
- Closed: possible answers to these are few and often predictable. They will not get a discussion going but are useful in verifying what has been said, thought or done.
- Open: this will draw an answer beyond yes and no and is the best method of developing discussion. The more open the question, the greater the quantity and quality of information offered. These questions will begin with: how, what, when, where, why, tell me about.
- Probing: a follow-up to the open question which enables the questioner to probe a specific area or develop an argument.

- Leading: this will attempt to gain the respondent's agreement with the speakers statement. Mostly used in interviews to test the attitudes and resolve of the applicant, but can be used provocatively in discussion.
- Multiple: a series of related questions. Answering this type of question was dealt with in the section on question handling. For the presenter, multiple questions can be a useful way of creating ignition at the start or to get discussion underway.

With the questions session successfully over, you are now ready to move into your summary (incorporating any vital issue that may have arisen during questions) and your final memorable statement. You are firmly back in control and a forceful ending will ensure that it is your message and not the questions that stay in the listeners' mind. (This aspect is covered in Chapter 4 on preparation.)

Exercise

Look at your speech and think of the questions you should, could or may be asked. Prepare your answers and be ready to use them when you rehearse with an audience.

Summary

The question and answer session is a major part of your speech and requires careful planning to minimize the loss of control. Retain control easily by following the question-answering sequence:

- Listen to make sure you understand the question.
- Acknowledge. Say "thank you" but do not patronize by saying things such as "that was an excellent question" unless you really mean it.
- Decide what type of question it is.
- Answer the question.
- Confirm that you have closed the gap by asking: "Does that help/answer/clarify?"
- Move on.
- Listen – pause – don't patronize – keep the answer short and sharp – close the knowledge gap.

7

Fine tuning for specific occasions
Final thoughts

Tips for different presentation scenarios

Summary

Fine tuning for specific situations

This book has concentrated mainly on the process of preparing and delivering a formal presentation. To deal successfully with the various types of briefings used in today's workplace may need a change of emphasis or some adjustments to the basic techniques used for formal presentations.

Outlined below are some of the issues which require special attention to cover such specific situations as: formal presentations; informal presentations; briefings; one-to-one presentations; workshops; meetings; telephone. Let us look at each in turn under the headings used throughout this book: preparation; delivery; aids; questions; equipment and location.

FORMAL: large audience
Preparation
- Follow the complete process.
- Make plenty of time for preparation and rehearsal.
- Seek advice and help from colleagues and friends.

Delivery
- Speed: let the sound carry and be careful not to speak too quickly.
- Volume: make sure you can be heard at the back of the room. during rehearsal, rather than at the start of the speech. Have a "plant" to signal if you are too loud or too soft.

- Pause: accentuate the pause in a large room.

Aids
- High quality.
- Easily seen.
- Use monitor screens if necessary.

Questions
- Who is handling them – you or the chairperson?
- Do you need to "plant" someone to ask questions?

Equipment/Location
- Visit location and check kit some days beforehand.
- Note position of equipment and issue instructions for any changes you need for your session.
- Check lectern height. Can you adjust it to your height?

INFORMAL: small group
Nowadays most presentations are informal and given to relatively small groups who are encouraged to become involved and participate as much as possible. In the business context, the format and the audience may still appear formal but every attempt is made to establish an informal atmosphere and style. The speaker must not relax his guard though, because in many ways it is a greater challenge to achieve an informal style while ensuring you remain completely alert and in control.

Preparation
- It is impressive to find out who is attending put names to faces.
- Study the individuals and discover what their particular responsibilities and interests are.
- Decide how much interaction you want and the best way to engineer it.
- Ensure at the start that you are focusing on the group's need by reconfirming what it is.
- Will you stand or sit? Can you lean/sit on a table to create a relaxed style but maintain good control?

Delivery
- RSVPP (scc p29): a good rhythm and pace is important and ensures that informality does not result in a dull over-soft tone.
- As you are close to your listeners and your body language, particularly your facial expressions can be easily picked up, maintaining a cheerful enthusiasm with good eye contact is important.

Aids
- Flip-charts, blackboard and scrolled OHP are less formal than pre-prepared slides and OHP – it depends how informal you wish to be!
- For groups of four or less, a briefing folder instead of screen-based aids effectively creates an atmosphere of informality.

Questions
- Allocate plenty of time.
- Decide whether ask for questions after each topic or at the end.
- Estimate how much time you can allow for the different topics.
- Summarize at the end of each topic. Relate to your main themes and aim.
- Be determined to stay in control despite the relaxed style.

Location
- Create a seating plan in which everyone can easily see each other and no-one dominates.
- Make sure there is plenty of space if you intend to form people into small groups for discussions.
- Use a room that fits the numbers attending. It is difficult to create informality if six people are in a 30-seat boardroom.

BRIEFINGS
Briefings usually cover a specific issue and are designed to tell people about a process or an activity. They are usually short affairs and often take place within a larger meeting.

Preparation
- Your script must be very tight, to the point and clearly signposted.

Delivery
- RSVPP: make sure you pause frequently to give time for your message to sink in.

Fine tuning for specific situations

- Seek frequent confirmation that your case is being understood.
- Keep to your outline script to ensure a crisp delivery.

Aids
- Use in sequence to explain process or system.
- Clarify each stage before moving to the next.

Questions
- Deal with the questions you are asked, then ask your audience questions to give them the chance to show they understood your briefing.

Location
- This is dependent on the size of your audience.

ONE-TO-ONE
Although these are probably the most frequent presentation occasions, they do not usually "count" as public speaking. Because of this many speakers do not experience the same dismay that they feel when faced with a larger audience. Even so all the basic presentation skills are required and the speech must be delivered in a personal conversational style.

Preparation
- Be absolutely clear why you are meeting and what the aim of both participants is.

- Find out as much as possible about the other "one", if you are a studier of psychological types. Adapt your style to suit your listener.
- Be prepared for a fluid agenda. List your bullet points on a sheet of paper and refer to it from time to time to check that you are covering them.Or, make your checklist points on a small card, place it in your pocket and check it toward the end of the session.
- Note down bullet points made by the other participant.

Delivery
- RSVPP: your conversational tone must still have vigour and enthusiasm, but should be designed to appeal to the other party's style.
- Develop your case as a conversation, pausing to allow an interjection.

Aids
- Use a briefing folder with a hard copy of your slides, but continue to use blank sheets to split up topics and to ensure your listener is focusing on you.

Questions
- Run your meeting as a discussion and keep asking your listener's opinion on your points. Wherever possible gain agreement to each stage as you go along.

Equipment/Location

- Make sure the room has an intimate, relaxed atmosphere and is private. It may make the other person feel safer if it is on their home ground or neutral territory.
- Decide whether the aim can more easily be achieved by a discussion over lunch or at a business meeting. If it is over lunch do not use aids, unless you can draw freehand on the menu card or a paper napkin!
- All you need is your briefing file and a summary note to take away.

WORKSHOP

At a workshop you expect your audience to participate and do much of the work. Your contribution is broken down into a series of mini presentations followed by group discussion and sometimes suggestions for solutions. Therefore, control and a quiet determination to return to your main themes as appropriate are important.

Preparation

- Be clear on the format of the session and which parts should be worked by you and which by the participants.
- Make sure you have solutions to the problems you set them.
- Think about the time needed for the different topics and build in plenty of spare for the overrun when the going gets interesting.
- Consider the individuals and whether seating can be ad hoc or should be organized to promote more successful group work.
- Making an interesting start and finish to each topic is very important, as well as introducing and summarizing the group work sessions.

Delivery

- All aspects of RSVPP are required.
- During discussion periods make sure you allocate your time fairly between groups.

Aids

- Provide flip-charts and markers for each group.
- Make sure your visuals can be seen by all groups.

Questions

- Take care to maintain control and make sure that intergroup rivalry contributes to rather than damages the outcome.
- Ensure fair exposure to all groups and try to involve individuals being crowded out by the extroverts.

Equipment/Location

- Make sure the room and tables are large enough for ease of movement and sight lines.
- Issue flip charts before the workshop starts.

Fine tuning for specific situations

MEETINGS

Meetings provide most of us with the greatest number of presentation opportunities even though they are usually short mini-statements. Regrettably, failure to plan before the meeting often results in disappointment for both speaker and listeners.

Preparation

- Work out in advance the topics you will be expected or may be invited to speak on (checking the agenda helps if there is one).
- Prepare your mini-presentation on these topics.
- Don't be satisfied with talking off the cuff because everyone else does.
- Prepare and rehearse a short snappy comment which lifts the standard of the meeting.
- Think about how you will attract the chairperson's attention to get the opportunity to say your piece. (It is sometimes necessary to warn him beforehand.)
- Tell another meeting member what you are going to say and get their agreement to support you.

Delivery

- RSVPP (p29) as appropriate for the size of the meeting.
- Body language is constrained because you are sitting down so make good eye contact and give verbal and facial support to other speakers so they do the same for you. If you want to make an impact, and you have the nerve, stand up to make your point and take control of that part of the meeting. Then sit down promptly afterwards.

Aids

- If the meeting room has a flip-chart or screen use it or, as a second best, distribute handouts.
- Probably your most useful aid will be you, so check and rehearse your preparation and delivery.

Questions

- Decide whether it will be you or the chairperson who will call for questions and control any discussion – do not take over the chair!
- Meetings are often a good opportunity for you to ask a question. A well-prepared and rehearsed question is short, to the point and makes an impact; a spur of the moment, ill-prepared one does not. Why take the risk?

Equipment/Location

- If you have been asked to speak and you know that a picture will make all the difference to the team's understanding of the issue, arrange for a flip-chart or OHP.
- If you can, ensure you are sitting near the chairperson and monitor his reaction to your comments.

TELEPHONE

This frequently and often poorly used method of presentation is usually covered in depth in books on telephone skills.

Preparation

- If it is an important call it needs preparation before delivery! Make a list of bullet points before the call.
- Prepare as you would for a face to face meeting.
- Book the call ahead of time so that your caller is ready for you.

Delivery

- Rely on your RSVPP (p29) and your question-handling techniques.
- Keep acknowledging your caller's points by saying something or grunting.
- The psychologists are adamant that a smiling cheerful caller transmits this to the listener.

Aids

- Before you call fax or e-mail any visuals that will help. Check they have arrived and are on your caller's desk.

Location

- Make sure there are no interruptions from any source.

VIDEO CONFERENCING

This means of communicating is increasing rapidly and can be used for all types of meeting from formal large groups, to one-to-one discussions.

Preparation

- Decide the type of session and prepare appropriately.

Delivery

- RSVPP but do not make sudden gestures or movements.
- Ensure your body language remains positive even when you're not speaking.

Aids

- Make sure you know how to send any aids or supporting material.

Location/Equipment

- Rehearsal using the system is essential for you or any colleagues unfamiliar with it.

Summary

The purpose of emphasizing specific points for the various types of presentation is simply to highlight their particular requirements and not to replace the more detailed comments made in the earlier chapters. Every presentation task is different and requires its own assessment and preparation.

Conclusion

This short book has outlined the various processes that lead to effective verbal communications. While there is little new to say on this subject I have tried to stress that, although the process helps to structure the preparation and delivery, the personality and style of the presenter are vital to the success of the presentation. We should not attempt to change or distort our personality but use it to make our case to others whether in one-to-one environment or at a large conference.

Presentation skill is just plain YOU, but you can make best use of your natural communication abilities to present effectively by being aware of and practising the tips outlined in this book. Remember the ten major points:

- MAKE SURE you (and your boss) are clear on the AIM.
- ASK THE SIX Qs: who? – what? – why? – when? – where? – how?
- STRUCTURE your presentation; have an EXCITING START, a LOGICAL MIDDLE and a MEMORABLE END.
- KEEP IT SIMPLE with no more than three main themes and two or three supporting points for each.

- WORK OUT in advance answers to possible QUESTIONS.
- DESIGN AIDS to support and enhance your case and do not detract from the most important aid – YOU.
- PREPARE memo cards with key words, instructions and reminders and with your opening and ending in full.
- REMEMBER RSVPP (p29).
- REHEARSE. Make a preparation plan with time to REHEARSE and PRACTISE.
- REVIEW your performance after the event and note what to do more of, less of and stop doing next time.

I was tempted to include something about controlling your nerves during the build up but, having focused on these tips with a variety of people, I know that the self-confidence generated by following them dispenses with the worries about nerves!

In the business context, to be effective, the "perfect" presentation should be professionally delivered, informative, well structured and enjoyable for all concerned. I trust that you are now better prepared to achieve this.

Index

Further reading

A brief visit to any business bookshop will reveal a large number of books on this subject. The choice of which to read rests on which style appeals to you most. These vary from the cartoon-laden and punchy to the more complete, serious and factual. After a glance at a few you will quickly get a feel for the style that suits you, not only for the initial read but also for future reference. Naturally I hope that the style of this book will suit most people, but if you wish to develop your skills even further I would recommend the following:

High Impact Business Presentations: Lee Bowman (Business Books Ltd, 1991)

Winning Presentations: David Gilgrist (Gower Publishing Ltd, 1996)

In addition two Video Arts booklets which accompany their training films on visual aids give excellent coverage on the detail of visual preparation:

Choosing and Using Charts: Gene Zelazny (Video Arts, 1972)

Slide Rules: Anthony Jay (Video Arts, 1976)

Printed and bound by Chorus-France